Australian Biographical Monographs

8

Australian Biographical Monographs
Series Editor: Scott Prasser

Previous Volumes

1

Joseph Lyons and the Management of Adversity
Kevin Andrews

2

Harold Holt and the Liberal Imagination
Tom Frame

3

Johannes Bjelke-Petersen
Bruce Kingston

4

Lindsay Thompson
Character, Competence and Conviction
William Westerman

5

Neville Wran
David Clune

6

Robert Menzies: Man or Myth
Scott Prasser

7

Stanley Melbourne Lee: Institution Builder
David Lee

Australian Biographical Monographs

8

John Grey Gorton
Australian to the Bootheels

Paul Williams

Connor Court Publishing

Published in 2020 by Connor Court Publishing Pty Ltd

Copyright © Paul Williams 2020

All rights reserved. No part of this book may be reproduced or transmitted in any form or by any means, electronic or mechanical, including photo copying, recording or by any information storage and retrieval system, without prior permission in writing from the publisher.

Connor Court Publishing Pty Ltd
PO Box 7257
Redland Bay QLD 4165
sales@connorcourt.com
www.connorcourt.com
Phone 0497-900-685

Printed in Australia

ISBN: 9781922449269

Front cover design: Maria Giordano

Front cover picture: Wikimedia Commons

For Noel and Nita Williams
Two quintessential post-war Australians

Australian Biographical Monographs

Series overview

The Connor Court Publishing's Australian Biographical Series on past leading Australian political leaders and other important figures seeks to provide an overview for those who are unfamiliar with the subject and to highlight the person's particular importance, controversies and contributions to Australia's progress.

The monographs are scholarly rather than academic in focus placing emphasis on a clear narrative, but with careful attention to referencing to ensure views expressed are supported by appropriate sources and evidence.

The Series was initiated because of the decline in the study of Australian history at our schools and universities and the consequential lack of knowledge or even worse, distorted views of some of Australia's leading figures who deserve to be remembered, understood for both their achievements, and as each volume also highlights, their flaws.

This new monograph on Australian Prime Minister Sir John Gorton (1968-71) by Dr Paul Williams, Senior Lecturer in politics, journalism and public relations at Griffith University's School of Humanities, Languages and Social Sciences, is more than just a snapshot of one of Australia's more interesting, and at times, most difficult to understand prime ministers. Rather, Dr Williams's considerable additional research provides a better understanding of the political context of Gorton's times. We come to appreciate the changing nature of Australian politics and society, including Labor's resurgence and the fracturing of the Liberal Party's dominance, and how each of these affected Gorton's prime ministership and assessments of his performance. Dr Williams has published widely on voter behaviour and political leadership in Australian scholarly journals, and he is a frequent commentator on Australian federal and Queensland state politics in the news media.

"We had reached a stage where we were on top of a mountain and we had to decide whether we stayed up there or go out in various directions…"

John Grey Gorton, 1998

INTRODUCTION:

JOHN GORTON AS A POLITICAL AND PERSONAL PARADOX?

Few familiar with the life and career of John Grey Gorton could deny the personal and professional complexity of Australia's 19th prime minister.

It is well known, for example, that Gorton was born out of wedlock at a time of great shame over illegitimacy. But lesser known is the question of whether Gorton was born in Australia or New Zealand or that, as a young boy, he was sent to live with his father's first wife after his mother died. Then there is the paradox of John Grey's upper-middle class background, including his attendance at exclusive schools, despite his father's mercurial income. The young Gorton was also highly intelligent yet scored mixed academic results.

Gorton's proud Australian nationalism is also well established, but less so his deep respect for Britain or his education at the University of Oxford. And while the adult Gorton boasted a strong Australian accent, his speech was occasionally punctuated by the long vowel of Received Pronunciation that saw him speak of "Orstralia". Nonetheless, Gorton insisted he was "Australian to the bootheels" – a deliberate, even provocative, contrast to Liberal Party founder Robert Menzies' boast of being "British to the bootheels". Moreover, the usually articulate Gorton was lampooned for speeches too often weighed down by meandering sentences. And while most regarded the man as genuinely amiable, John Grey could also be sharply sarcastic.

The contradictions continued when Gorton graduated from

Oxford and returned to Australia as a modest Victorian orchardist. In 1940, John Grey volunteered for military pilot training. After the war, he won election to the local shire before being elected to the Senate in 1949. Beginning public life as an avowed anti-communist 'hawk', Gorton evolved into a moderate 'dove' and self-described 'owl'.[1] On social policy, Gorton also championed civil liberties, the arts, the environment, the rights of women and of Gay Australians – and later supported drug and abortion law reform – and was committed to improving conditions among Indigenous communities. Gorton, an overtly masculine figure who excelled at sport and who loved a drink, a smoke and a party, also preferred the company of women, and sought their political advice at a time when few were held in such esteem.

The paradoxes continued for a man who worked diligently in junior ministries – Navy, Interior, Works, Education and Science – but who remained largely unknown outside Canberra before becoming a candidate, in December, 1967, to replace the drowned Harold Holt as prime minister. Indeed, it was unusual for a party leader to rise from minor portfolios, and wholly unprecedented for one to emerge from the Senate. Moreover, after working hard for a prime ministership he clearly coveted, Gorton adopted a casual approach to the job's day to day demands.

The conflict between the public and private Gortons extended to the arts. While John Grey publicly "delighted in the role of the no-nonsense philistine", privately he was "well-read" and an anonymously published poet.[2] Ultimately, despite occupying safe Liberal Party berths in both the Senate and House of Representatives – and despite membership of the exclusive Melbourne Club –

Gorton avowed he was "not of or in the establishment".[3] Inevitably, Gorton's unorthodox style and rejection of many conservative shibboleths saw him derided by journalists and pilloried by colleagues, many of whom blamed Gorton personally for the Coalition's near-defeat at the 1969 federal election.

Deconstructing Gorton's political philosophy is therefore critical to locating the man's place in Australian history. But it is also problematic. While Gorton demonstrated many traits in common with utilitarian liberal philosopher John Stuart Mill[4], he falls short of being labelled a genuine 'social liberal'. And while John Grey adopted a number of conservative positions, especially in foreign policy early in his career, the man could never be called a 'conservative' in the Burkean tradition. Given his wildly varying and sometimes contradictory philosophies, we can at least say 'Gortonism' – a complex term anatomised in Chapter Five – comprised something of a 'variegated' liberalism.

Yet that none of that mitigates the problem of Gorton being little acknowledged and even less understood in Australian history. But this paucity of recognition has not curbed scholarly attempts at rating the efficacy of his prime ministership.

In 1992, a *Canberra Times* survey of 143 Australian political scientists rated Gorton 12th among 19 prime ministers, immediately below Edmund Barton and immediately above Joe Lyons, and five places above Harold Holt and six above McMahon.[5] In 2001, the *Australian Financial Review* rated Gorton 16th from 21 candidates, one below Chris Watson, one above Holt, and five places above McMahon as lowest rated.[6] In 2004, *The Age* ranked the 11 prime ministers from

John Curtin to John Howard and placed Gorton ninth, one above Holt and two above the lowest ranked McMahon.[7] Similarly, a 2010 Monash University survey ranked Gorton 16th from 23 leaders, one place below Stanley Bruce, one above Kevin Rudd, two above Holt and seven places above McMahon[8]. In 2013, veteran psephologist Malcom Mackerras rated Gorton 17th from 26: one place below Holt, one above Watson and eight ahead of McMahon.[9]

There are, of course, numerous references to Gorton in any number of political histories and compendia of Australian prime ministers. And while John Grey wrote three short but significant scholarly works – on the Liberal Party, on federalism, and on the role of the prime minister[10] - he wrote no autobiography. The closest he came was a 1971 series of six long newspapers articles for *The Sunday Australian*.

That leaves just three books exclusively on Gorton. The first is Alan Trengrove's *John Grey Gorton: An Informal Bibliography*[11], published in 1969 and the first public acknowledgement of the circumstances of John Grey's birth. This book offers great insight into Gorton's early life but its venture into hagiography limits its utility. The second is *The Gorton Experiment*[12], a vitriolic account published in 1971 by a Packer press journalist, Alan Reid, known for his support of Gorton rival McMahon. Three decades passed before Gorton received his most substantial treatment in Ian Hancock's *John Gorton: He did it his way*. This book – also sympathetic – emerged amid new public interest in a most unorthodox prime minister. Just months before its publication, Gorton had turned 90 before being formally acknowledged by a Liberal Party, via a gala celebratory dinner, he had rejoined in 1999. In the presence of Prime

Minister John Howard, Gorton again received peer approval: the paradoxical John Grey had come full circle.

Why, then, another book on Gorton? First, this is the first substantial work published on Gorton since his death almost two decades ago. Second, this book – while following a roughly linear history – comprises a leadership analysis, and cites unpublished personal communications between John Grey and myself. Third, there remain three fresh fields in which assessments of Gorton's place in Australian history can be made. The first is historiographical: is history right to paint his leadership in such poor light, especially regarding the man's role in the Coalition's near-defeat in 1969? The second is ideological: what is 'Gortonism' and how has it shaped Australian liberal thought and practice? The third is operational: does Gorton's leadership, while unconventional, offer any lessons today?

This book does not seek to canonise a flawed public and private figure. But it does offer three arguments. The first is that popular histories are wrong to apportion near-total blame to Gorton for the Coalition's 1969 result. The second is that Gorton was not an inert 'place holder' inexpediently wedged between Menzies and Whitlam, nor merely a 'transactional' leader geared only to win re-election. Instead, I argue 'Gortonism' was an attempt at genuinely 'transformational' leadership in which Gorton sought to steer Australia from an essentially British small 'c' conservative nation into a proudly Australian small 'l' liberal democracy. As such, Gorton's ideological leadership served as a cultural bridge between Menzies' liberal conservatism and Whitlam's social democracy. It must be noted, however, that Gorton's predecessor Holt constructed his own part of this bridge with such liberal reforms as an initial dismantling of the White Australia Policy, new Commonwealth control (via the 1967 referendum) over Indigenous affairs, the introduction of decimal currency (with the 'Dollar' and not a 'Royal' as the denomination), the establishment of a National Gallery and an Australia Council for the Arts, and an engagement with Asia in foreign policy.

Third, I argue Gorton was not a 'great' prime minister as Alfred Deakin, John Curtin or Robert Menzies might be so described. Indeed, Mackerras' description of Gorton as a "lower average" leader appears appropriate. But John Grey's ability to harness a new Australian nationalism, and his delivery of substantial, if few, liberal reforms over just 38 months must surely rate him higher than 'poor' overall. But I also argue Gorton's specific operational leadership was indeed 'poor', and certainly fell short of that required of a prime minister overseeing rapid economic and cultural change. Consequently, these shortcomings see Gorton's overall prime ministership most accurately ranked as 'mediocre'.

This book comprises eight sections. The first explores Gorton's place in history. This is followed by a snapshot of Gorton's youth, education and war service – assessed via rudimentary psycho-biographical theory – that draws links between a younger Gorton's formative experiences and a mature politician's paradoxical style. Sections Three and Four then analyse Gorton's backbench and ministerial careers as the progenitors of 'Gortonism', while Sections Five and Six analyse Gorton's prime ministership via his ideological and operational leadership respectively. Section Seven then summarises the events during and after Gorton's exit from public life before Section Eight draws critical conclusions.

1

GORTON AS A PROBLEM OF HISTORY

John Grey Gorton presents something of a problem for Australian history. On the one hand, few Australians under a certain age would recognise Gorton's name or distinctive face despite his prime ministership, beginning in early 1968, coinciding with a new phase in the reporting of politics in the Australian news media. That lack of recognition might be explained by Gorton's unfortunate timing as a prime minister – with Harold Holt, Jack McEwen and Billy McMahon – squeezed between the retirement of one political leviathan, Sir Robert Menzies in January, 1966, and the coming of another, Labor's Gough Whitlam, in December, 1972.

On the other hand, if Gorton is remembered at all it is likely for superficial reasons: a 'Jolly John' party image of a gregarious man who enjoyed the company of women – including his young private secretary Ainsley Gotto – a lackadaisical approach to his prime ministerial duties, and the unique way in which Gorton removed himself from office. But these recollections are reductionist and tell us little about the man's ideological or operational leadership.

That's why Gorton – prime minister between 9 January, 1968, and 10 March, 1971 – also presents something of a problem for historiography. Like most political leaders, opinion is divided over Gorton's efficacy as prime minister. But, unlike most, opinion of Gorton is especially imbalanced.

Perhaps the most enduring impression is that Gorton was the sole or principal architect of the Liberal-Country Party (LCP) Coalition's near-defeat, after suffering a record 7.1 per cent two party-preferred (2PP) swing, at the 1969 federal election: a poll that paved the way for a Whitlam-led Labor Party to terminate, in December, 1972, a 23-year Coalition hegemony. That consensus for blame began before the 1969 election when, just weeks before the October poll, the Liberal and later Independent MP for Warringah (NSW), Edward St John – a fierce Gorton critic – argued that

> if in the upshot the Labor Party makes any substantial gains [in the poll] it will not be due to any particular merit on its part. *It will be due rather to the character and conduct of Mr Gorton*, as he now stands revealed… [emphasis added].[13]

But perhaps the most readily accepted view of Gorton's role in the Coalition's 1969 result – and of Gorton's allegedly poor leadership generally – came from Packer journalist Alan Reid who, immediately after the 1969 election, wrote that Gorton was "the major factor in the coalition's reverse [sic]".[14] Reid continued this attack in *The Gorton Experiment*, his scornful 1971 account of the Gorton prime ministership that John Grey said was merely a "justification for [him] not to be Prime Minister".[15] Indeed, Reid struck at the very heart of historiography when he argued the "Gorton policies and style" produced "the pattern of the changing [election] figures in the Canberra school [on the] night of October 25, 1969".[16]

Even Liberal Prime Minister John Howard conceded that, in 1967, he "didn't want John Gorton to succeed Harold Holt". Indeed, Howard was:

> frustrated that a man of such high intelligence and personal appeal [as Gorton] displayed insufficient discipline, and sensitivity to those who mattered, to retain control of the prime ministership. The disappointment was that the leadership he might have given Australia never completely materialised.

By the 1990s Howard had warmed to Gorton – whom he labels the "Tory larrikin" – and he now concedes "some of [Gorton's] ideas had been ahead of their time".[17]

There are, however, a few who applaud Gorton's leadership, including John Grey himself who, in 1998, told me he was Australia's "best" prime minister.[18] Liberal Party co-founder Sir John Cramer was similarly disposed, declaring Gorton to be "really the best prime minister we ever had who was a truly Australian type".[19] The former Independent Tasmanian Senator Reg 'Spot' Turnbull agreed, describing Gorton as "the best of all the prime ministers". He also described as "absurd" claims that Gorton's leadership contributed to the 1969 result.[20] Former Liberal Minister and Australian Democrats founder Don Chipp concurred, arguing Gorton "would have been the greatest prime minister Australia ever had, but for the forces of evil – the conservatism that tore the Liberal Party apart…".[21]

These competing views can be read as something of a proxy battle in a wider historiographical war over a key question: to what extent can a single individual shape history? Is it, as the 'Great Man' theory attests, that history is made principally by single individuals through the sheer force of talent and personality alone? A. J. P. Taylor, for one, argued "the history of modern Europe can be written in terms of three titans: Napoleon, Bismarck, and Lenin".[22] Or is it, as

Karl Marx's 'historical materialism' contends, that history is shaped by a society's economic substructure from which individuals – as mere products of the prevailing economic forces – can rise to prominence only at critical junctures?[23] Or is history a serendipitous intersection of the two where historically significant individuals, necessarily boasting particular personal qualities, will find no traction until the broader socio-economic conditions are ripe?

The 1969 Federal Election: Gorton and the Forces of Change

The late 1960s saw a booming Australian economy with full employment, low inflation and rising household income. It was a sanguine mood matched by a burgeoning Australian nationalism as excitement soared over the country's biggest mineral boom since the 19th century gold rushes. Yet, despite this buoyancy, the Coalition in 1969 suffered a massive 2PP swing of more than seven per cent – the largest since 1931 – and the loss of 16 seats to Labor. As I have argued elsewhere,[24] Gorton's role in facilitating that swing – especially his unorthodox operational leadership – was not insubstantial. But Gorton's responsibility must be balanced with other factors influencing Australian voters during a period of rapid economic and cultural change.

Constraints prevent lengthy discussion here but a key factor beyond Gorton's control was a public rejection of the growing dissonance within and among the non-Labor parties – Liberals, the Country Party and the Democratic Labor Party (DLP) – as skirmishes erupted between social conservatives and liberals, defence 'hawks' and 'doves', and trade protectionists and free-traders. Second, in the 'zero-sum game' of Australian politics – where the loss of support from one side will be a commensurate gain for the other – the appeal of a modern and newly moderate Labor Party, led by the charismatic Gough Whitlam, became a major factor in that swing. Indeed, a Labor Party now offering material reform in health and education – and post-material reform for women, Indigenous Australians, migrants, the environment and the arts – appealed to a burgeoning white-collar middle class increasingly fatigued by a Coalition shackled to ancient shibboleths.

Third, Australia in the late 1960s saw the emergence of a freshly invigorated news media – accommodating a new class of young and assertive Canberra Press Gallery journalists such as Richard Carleton and Laurie Oakes – that saw television programs like the ABC's *This Day Tonight* not only report daily political events but critique the context in which they occurred.

A fourth factor is found in a changing Australian demography that included increasing numbers of migrants and the first voting cohort of baby-boomers born between 1946 and 1948 who demanded improved health, welfare and education services. Concomitantly, a fifth factor became the rapidly shifting external forces – increasing demands for human rights, environmentalism and peace as the Vietnam War soured and the communist 'threat' diminished – that saw voters gravitate toward social democratic parties at home and abroad.

This short book cannot unpack these factors. It can only deconstruct Gorton's life and career as one Australia's most unconventional political leaders.

2

DEPRIVATION, COMPENSATION AND WAR: THE MAKING OF A MAVERICK LEADER

While the date of John Grey Gorton's birth – 9 September, 1911 – is certain, exactly where he came into the world is not. Was it, as indicated on a birth certificate for a "John Alga Gordon" (Gordon was the latter name of one Alice Sinn, Gorton's biological mother) in Melbourne, Victoria? Or was it, as Gorton's father John Rose Gorton (John Rose traced his surname, Old English for "Dirty Town", to the 13th century[25]) had long told him, in Wellington, New Zealand: a location John Grey listed in applications to both Oxford and the Royal Australian Air Force?

And while there is no doubt John Grey was born out of wedlock, there is confusion over whether John Rose was ever married to John Grey's mother, Alice, the daughter of a railway worker. Indeed, we know John Rose remained married to Kitty O'Brien and, if he had married Alice, he was "almost certainly a bigamist".[26] In any event, John Rose – a Boer War profiteer, night club owner and orchardist – earned a reputation as something of a "scoundrel".[27]

John Grey had just one sibling: a sister, Ruth, two years' his senior, who "gave the impression of thinking she was better than her brother".[28] Moreover, John Rose appeared emotionally closer to Ruth than to his son. Ruth lived with Kitty and, astonishingly, John Grey first met his sister years after being told she had died.

Youth and Education

A core element in Gorton's political socialisation appeared to emerge from his childhood exposure to a blend of conservatism and social liberalism. While his father was a "conservative" and "unashamed capitalist",[29] John Grey's formative years came during a bold liberal experiment in which Labor Prime Minister Andrew Fisher employed Commonwealth power to legislate on social security, industrial relations, land monopolies, and the power to establish such proudly Australian institutions as the Australian Navy, the Commonwealth Bank and an Australian national currency. A maturing Gorton – growing up during the 'flaming youth' of a liberal 1920s[30] – was surely cognisant of these reforms.

This existential duality continued for John Grey as the young boy's living arrangements alternated between the opulent Menzies Hotel and the working-class Port Melbourne home of his maternal grandparents. It is further illustrated in an incident Gorton loved to re-tell: at age six, the boy badly injured his knee, and he was admitted to a public ward where he enjoyed the company of working class men.

Tragically, Gorton's mother – whom John Grey described as "very, very attractive"[31] – died from tuberculosis in 1920, aged 32, when the boy was just nine years old. And while the young Gorton had grown accustomed to his parents' frequent absences, his grief from maternal loss can only have been enormous. But the mature Gorton dismissed this childhood trauma and insisted he "just got on with it".[32] Historian Gerard Henderson agrees, arguing Gorton survived childhood relatively unscathed and that the boy, "compared with many of his generation…did not have a tough life".[33] If true in terms of Gorton's material environment, it was almost certainly untrue of his emotional development.

Gorton's principal biographers are convinced the young John was permanently scarred by childhood loss. Trengrove, for example, argued that:

> [i]n his tender years Gorton was moved from one environment to another, and now at seven [sic] years of age he was passed from the control of one woman to another...The effect on him must surely have been insecurity, and if this is so, it perhaps explains his innate suspiciousness and his nonchalant cynicism of a man who has known deep hurt and needs a tough shell.[34]

Hancock agreed when he argued that:

> [i]t is certainly true he developed a hard exterior... John Gorton was fiercely competitive, was determined always to win, rarely backed down in an argument, and never backed away from a fight. Nevertheless, inside was someone quite shy, very sensitive, easily offended, eager to please, and looking for acknowledgment. The older John Grey Gorton found it hard to trust others, and placed the highest value on loyalty. He carried with him into politics a genuine sympathy for the disadvantaged...At the same time, his own capacity to overcome hardship, and his eagerness to grasp opportunities, convinced him the meek should not inherit the earth.[35]

These descriptions point to an early gestation of a primary Gorton paradox: an idealist John Grey who – while sympathetic to those denied his own advantage – was nonetheless forced to reconcile with the pragmatism of helping oneself, just as he had done.

John Grey began his education at Sydney's prestigious Edgecliff Preparatory School then, on the death of his mother, John Rose sent the boy across town to live with Kitty. In no time at all, Gorton had effectively lost both parents. Gorton then attended Headfort College and, at age 12, the exclusive Sydney Church of England Grammar School – his classmates included famous actor Errol Flynn and artist Russell Drysdale. He excelled at sports, but failed his Intermediate Certificate. At 15, Gorton returned to Victoria to attend the equally exclusive Geelong Grammar. Here, the popular and lanky John Grey, nicknamed 'Droop,' assumed school leadership positions. Interestingly, some of Geelong's left-leaning masters – including the Christian socialist headmaster James Darling who encouraged students to collect food for the underprivileged – later described Gorton as "wilful and reckless." But they also managed to instil in the boy a love of community service, political debate and history.[36] Indeed, Gorton came to identify with Abraham Lincoln, the 16th American President, who had also lost his mother at a tender age.

On matriculation, Gorton worked for a year on his father's orchard before enrolling at Brasenose College at Oxford University to read economics, politics and history. His years there appear to have been critical in wedding liberal social values to a nascent anti-communist dogma. While at Oxford, Gorton took flying lessons, gained his pilot's licence at aged 20, and captained the rowing team. He also had his first sexual experience at this time: an illicit relationship with an older married woman.[37] But a popular Gorton still often felt an outsider at Oxford given his poverty relative to other students.

Indeed, John Grey appeared to form few strong male friendships at Oxford but one, with John Buchan, proved memorable after the pair shared a fortnight's holiday on a fishing boat with working class Yorkshire men. Another was with the American Arthur Brown whose 18 year old sister, Bettina, had caught John's eye while holidaying in Spain. John and Betty married impulsively in early 1935 and, even here, Gorton broke convention: he told the rector Betty was 21, and he failed to secure his college's requisite permission before marriage.

Gorton graduated Master of Arts in 1935 and, on returning to Australia, he sat – and failed – the Department of External Affairs examination. While Gorton pondered a career in journalism, or possibly the diplomatic service, John Rose died and, in 1936, his son inherited a debt-ridden orchard. John and Betty returned to the farm and thereafter "dreaded receiving mail because of the constant requests from banks and creditors for repayment".[38] This new, tough life of a Mallee farmer again allowed Gorton to identify as an Australian 'underdog'.

War and Insouciance

If these experiences were the bricks in the political socialisation of a future prime minister, Gorton's war years were the mortar. As a student, Gorton had lived in Britain and watched first-hand as local fascists championed the far right in Germany, Italy and Spain. He had also seen the brutality of Stalinist Russia. It is therefore unsurprising the liberal Gorton's loathing of totalitarianism should cultivate his anti-communism.

On war's outbreak in 1939, Gorton heard the call to serve despite being almost 30, a married father of two, and working in an 'essential industry'. He was, after all, a qualified pilot. On 31 May, 1940, Gorton drove to Swan Hill to enlist in the Royal Australian Air Force Reserve. His request to fly bemused recruiters who saw an older and seemingly uneducated hick dressed in shabby farm clothes. His Oxford degree and pilot's licence soon changed their minds.

Gorton's speech at his farewell party was long remembered by locals, if only as one indicative of a developing world view: "Things would not be permitted to sink back again to the pre-war state of existence," John Grey said. "There must be a new order, one that will take the place of the old order permanently".[39]

Gorton, now a father of three, was awarded his military wings on 1 May, 1941, and he later trained on Tiger Moth aircraft in Australia and on Spitfires and Hurricanes in England. The Allies were now at war with Japan, and Gorton was posted to Singapore to assist in its defence. In late January, 1942, Gorton's Hurricane was attacked by a Japanese Zero and, when John Grey crashed his bullet-ridden plane on Bintairn Island, his face slammed into the instrument panel. His broken nose and two crushed cheek bones were rudimentarily repaired but Gorton had to wait till mid-February before scheduled repatriation to a New Zealand hospital. On route, his transport ship was torpedoed, and survivors scrambled onto rafts. They floated in the sea for a night and day before rescue.

Gorton was back in Australia by mid-1942 and was soon posted to Western Australia, then to Milne Bay, New

Guinea, where he mentored younger flyers. It was at this time Gorton suffered a third near-death experience when he crashed his plane off Melville Island near Darwin. Alone, Gorton survived there for days on turtle eggs.[40] John Grey's fourth brush with death came in March, 1943, when he again walked away from yet another serious crash. The wearied pilot had now "had enough" and he relinquished active service for a posting to Townsville, and then to Mildura, as a flying instructor.[41]

Despite Gorton in late 1944 undergoing plastic surgery on his face, the still youngish man's visage would remain craggily disfigured. He would be later described as "attractively ugly"[42] and as "the Liberal with a Labor supporter's face".[43] Either way, the physical scars of war must surely have changed the way he believed the world saw a once handsome man. The RAAF discharged Gorton as Flight Lieutenant in December, 1944, and John Grey returned to his struggling Victorian orchard and his role as a "distant yet benevolent father".[44]

He would always scoff at suggestions he was a hero.

A Theory…

Psychobiography – where the disciplines of psychology and biography meet to determine how public figures are shaped – suffers a chequered history.[45] On the one hand, psychobiography offers plausible explanations as to why certain individuals and not others seek political office, and why they lead the way they do. Adolf Hitler's brutality, for example, is usefully attributed to a violent father, while United States President Woodrow Wilson's ambition is sheeted home to a childhood dyslexia and the quest for paternal approval.

But psychobiography is also an inexact science requiring a degree of speculation. It is therefore criticised for potentially flimsy methodologies, for over-simplifying subjects' complex cognitive processes, and for expediently 'retro-fitting' adult behaviours to childhood experiences. While acknowledging the limits of psychobiography, this chapter employs – at a rudimentary level given space constraints – one of the discipline's core theories: the impact of childhood deprivation and an adult need for to compensate for loss to link young and mature behaviours.

Drawing on the early work of Sigmund Freud, American political scientist Harold Lasswell argued personal insecurities can be traced to whether the child was indulged in prosperity or deprived in adversity and, further, that unresolved insecurities in adults can be displaced onto "political objects".[46] Lasswell thereafter explored the "political type" – he coined the term *homo politicus* – to argue certain childhood experiences require compensation in adult life. Importantly, Lasswell argued the need for compensation can produce public, and especially political, persons: "to overcome low estimates of the self", a political aspirant "pursues power as a means of compensation against deprivation".[47] Lasswell further argued the "political type" is "characterized by an intense and ungratified craving for deference": a need for the respect of others, and for the attendant feelings of superiority such respect can bring. This emotional need for deference, Lasswell argued, is specifically rooted in an individual's "displacement" of "private motives" (a need to be admired) onto "public objects" (the people). Indeed, Lasswell derived a scientific equation where **(p)** represents a political aspirant's "private motives" for public life, **(d)** represents the displacement of that individual's childhood deprivation (of love, attention or other need) onto public audiences, and **(r)** represents that individual's need to "rationalize" that displacement – and their role in public life – often through ideological dogma. It stands that **(P)** becomes the sum of those forces to produce a particular "political type":[48] **p } d } r = P**

This thesis has been widely adopted across political science, with the esteemed leadership scholar James Macgregor Burns drawing on Lasswell to posit his "wellsprings of want" theory.[49]

...And its Application

This theory allows us to draw several plausible links between Gorton's formative experiences – childhood, youth, education and war – and his paradoxical ideology and unorthodox operational leadership.

First, Gorton's experiences prior to public life can be dichotomised into Internal and External influences. In terms of the Internal, evidence points to an array of early experiences that, in turn, produced three distinct effects on the maturing Gorton. While, for example, the boy's illegitimate birth would have inculcated a sense of difference (but not necessarily embarrassment) in young John, his mercurial domestic circumstances – regular stays with his grandparents and moving between Sydney and Melbourne – would have created physical insecurities. More important, however, is the likelihood that John Grey's frequently absent parents, his emotionally distant father and, most critically, the death of his beloved mother and relocation to an emotionally distant step-mother, could only have filled an already lonely boy with even greater emotional hunger.

These effects appear to have manifested in several Gorton traits: an ignorance of – or even disregard for – social conventions that, in turn, produced a seemingly brusque or arrogant manner; an aloof independence and an insistence on assuming control of one's own destiny; an inherent suspicion of others in an uncertain world where loved ones can be so easily snatched away; and – according to 'deprivation-compensation' theory – a displacement of these needs onto external objects to gain the love and respect he so fiercely desired. Moreover, the theory also explains Gorton's preference for the company of women: affection, or at least attention, drawn from women was likely a subconscious quest to replace a lost mother's love.

In terms of the External, the evidence suggests the young Gorton's exposure to contradictory economic, social and political circumstances contributed to complex, even contradictory, world views. On the one hand, young John would have been conflicted over his need for acceptance among affluent boys at his exclusive schools with, on the other, love for his working class maternal grandparents and, later, his respect for the humble folk he met in Port Melbourne, in hospital and on a fishing boat. Later, John Grey would have been forced to reconcile the conservative capitalism of his father (whom he loved) with the humanist teachings of his school masters (whom he admired). The result appears to have been a conflicted Gorton forced to accommodate these internal contradictions via the adoption of a broad political philosophy, with a pragmatic John Grey oscillating between the ideological right and left as required. The maturing Gorton, for example, eagerly embraced the wealth-producing ethos of, first, the Country Party and, later, the Liberals. But Gorton – who had so often felt lonely and excluded – also empathised with society's marginalised members. It therefore appears inevitable that, notwithstanding early 'hawkish' anti-communist and anti-socialist rhetoric, Gorton should identify with the left of the Victorian Liberals and a range of progressive social policies.

There is strong evidence Gorton's war experiences were also a significant factor in the development of the mature politician. Studies have revealed, for example, that war veterans who suffer "psychological trauma and social dislocation" also find "new opportunities and potential for personal growth."[50] More specifically, it is also established that military service, where recruits come together from a range of socio-economic backgrounds to bond in adversity, can serve as a social and cultural equalizer.[51] Gorton's exposure to men of different walks of life, at a moment when character and skill mattered more than birthright, can only have sharpened his demand for equality.

Intuitively, Gorton's mature world view must also have been shaped by the four occasions on which he cheated death. Given the wide acceptance of the near-death experience as "usually transformational, causing enhanced intuitive sensibility, profound changes of life insight, and the loss of the fear of death," it is likely Gorton quickly overcame any number of youthful fears.[52] If we accept John Grey soon recognised he was now enjoying a life that could so easily have been lost, it is little wonder the man adopted after 1945 a degree of insouciance in his interpersonal relations.

If war did not kill him, nothing could.

3

FROM SHIRE TO SENATE

Unsurprising given his father's agricultural interests, Gorton joined the Country Party in the late 1930s. But war interrupted his political aspirations. By 1946, Gorton could no longer resist the call to public office. In April, John Grey wrote a potent speech – so carefully prepared it undermines later allegations of an always lackadaisical man – for a Welcome Home celebratory dinner in Mystic Park, Victoria, where he paid homage to servicemen and women. Here, we see an early acknowledgement of the need to improve economic and social conditions for women and not just men:

> We must remove from the minds of men the fear of poverty as the result of illness, or accident, or old age. We must turn our schools into institutions which will produce young men and women avid for further education and increased knowledge. We must raise the material standard of living so that all children can grow up with sufficient space and light and proper nourishment; so that women may be freed of domestic drudgery; and so that scientific inventions which are conducive to a more gracious life may be brought within the means of us all.[53]

First, Gorton's reference to eliminating poverty, to advancing education and science, and to the welfare of women suggests a progressive liberalism always ran through John Grey. Second, such a speech appears to have been critical preparation for a political career that was neither accidental nor reluctant. Indeed, Gorton was not drafted by others to serve in adversity; he actively sought public office as an ambitious example of Lasswell's *homo politicus*. Whether that ambition was for personal gratification to compensate for childhood deprivation or, more likely, motivated by a blend of private emotional need and public service altruism, John Grey would not die wondering. It surprised few, then, when Gorton announced his candidacy for a seat on the Kerang Shire Council in 1946. The fact no one else had nominated – and that Gorton was denied a battle on the hustings and was elected unopposed – must have fuelled the fire in his belly.

But Gorton was equally incensed by the Chifley Labor Government's easy re-election – despite Menzies launching an attractive new Liberal Party two years previously – at the 1946 poll. That election allowed Ben Chifley to pursue Labor's touchstone objective of bank nationalisation that, in turn, galvanised anti-Labor support across Australia's middle class. That policy certainly fired Gorton's ire but, interestingly, his greatest resentment came not from its socialist tenor but, instead, from the alleged gall of a parliament passing nation-changing legislation without consulting the people at referendum.[54]

The year 1947 was critical for Gorton. Those pushing for a united anti-socialist front against Labor, including Gorton, convinced the Liberals' Victorian division to absorb moderate Country Party members into a new Liberal and Country Party (LCP). The decision to change allegiance must have been difficult for a rural man who, like his father, identified strongly with the Country Party. But ambition and pragmatism undoubtedly forced John Grey's hand.

Gorton soon won LCP preselection for the Legislative Council's Northern Province at the 1947 state election. The fact he lost by around 300 votes in a safe Country Party district speaks not only to the LCP's growing influence in regional Victoria but also to John Grey's budding campaign skills. His defeat proved propitious: the ambitious Gorton could now set his sights higher than provincial politics despite his recent election in 1949 as Kerang Shire President.

Melbourne LCP powerbrokers were now aware of the rural firebrand, and they found a berth – third place on a joint LCP-Country Party Senate ticket – for him at the 1949 federal election. The change in 1948 in the Senate's electoral system, from Preferential to Single Transferable Vote, naturally enhanced Gorton's chances and, on 10 December, he was elected to the Senate. John Grey, sworn in as LCP Senator for Victoria on 22 February, 1950, brimmed with confidence. Asked what he thought of his newly-elected colleagues, he curtly replied, "Not much. I'm the best of them".[55]

Backbench

Gorton's years on the backbench, 1950 to 1958, underscore two points. First, Senator Gorton quickly earned a reputation for erudite and well-researched addresses. Again, this undermines later opinions that Gorton was always unprepared, or that he inevitably mangled the English language. Second, Gorton's early speeches contain the origins of later ideological hallmarks, and confirm that 'Gortonism' was not a haze of extempore ideas cobbled together after Holt's disappearance but, rather, a set of broad ideological principles refined over many years' parliamentary experience.

First, evidence of Gorton's vehement anti-communism is found in his maiden Senate speech in March, 1950:

> It may well be that the ominous shadow which is now creeping down through China, threatening Malaya and Indonesia and coming closer to the near north of this country, will reach us without warning and that we shall not have those months of preparation which last time were bought for us by the suffering and sacrifice of our kinsfolk in Britain.[56]

Gorton's anti-communist fervour inevitably framed his interest in defence policy more broadly, especially after Gorton joined – and later assumed the Chair of – the Joint Parliamentary Committee on Foreign Affairs. John Grey's anti-communism naturally made him fearful of Chinese Communist influence in the region after 1949 – he was an early supporter of the Southeast Asia Treaty Organisation (SEATO) – and he joined an informal cabal among foreign policy 'hawks' (with Jim Killen, W.C. Wentworth and Wilfred Kent-Hughes) supporting Australia's controversial deployment, in 1966, of an ambassador to Taiwan.[57]

Second, and paradoxically, Gorton's commitment to small 'l' liberal values appeared during the same *Communist Party Dissolution Bill* debate where he acknowledged Labor's concerns over a potential erosion of civil liberties. "The bill is not intended or designed to crush an idea," Gorton said. "The whole purpose of the bill [is] to prevent action and not to crush thought. You cannot impale an idea on the point of a bayonet".[58]

Yet, even here, Gorton sent mixed messages. He endorsed, for example, the gathering of intelligence on suspected communists and, during debate over federal police powers in 1957, argued that commencing Commonwealth Police officers be forced to swear an oath they were "not now and never have been a member of the Australian Communist Party".[59]

Gorton also sometimes defended workers' rights against business interests. During debate on a stevedoring bill in 1956, for example, John Grey declared that "one of the principal causes of [industrial relations] turbulence" in the industry "stem[med] from the earlier arrogant attitude of the shipowners".[60]

Third, early speeches also reflect John Grey's bold Australian nationalism. In addition to his advocacy of Australian atomic energy – and later the acquisition of nuclear weapons – Gorton argued for an Australian foreign policy independent of both Britain and the United States. And while John Grey in 1956 championed Australia's stake in Antarctica,[61] his economic nationalism emerged during that same year during debate on the *Australian Coastal Shipping Commission Bill* to establish a Commonwealth-owned shipping line.[62]

Early evidence is also found for Gorton's early support for an administrative centralism that ran contrary to the Liberals' traditional federalist model. During debate on the *Commonwealth Aid Roads Bill* in June, 1956, for example, John Grey argued "[a]ny legislation which will help to improve Australia's road system must be of advantage to the whole of this country". For Gorton, "the national outlook should always prevail".[63]

Last, we find ample evidence of Gorton's progressive conceptions of welfare and education spending. In 1952, John Grey touted the opportunities for increased public investment in education and, in 1957, the need to means-test age pensions.[64]

Despite his record, Gorton struggled to gain the approval of Menzies – whom he admired but never feared – from a backbench replete with equally talented, and far more compliant, new members. Gorton's penchant for 'Devil's Advocacy', for example, saw him frequently question Menzies in the party room, and his support for Labor amendments to the *Income Tax Assessment Bill* in 1952 annoyed the Prime Minister who called him a mischief-maker. Little surprise, then, that Gorton should be passed over for promotion.[65]

Interestingly, while Gorton developed a deep antipathy towards some Opposition MPs – West Australian Senator Don Willesee, for example – he also cultivated close and enduring friendships with, among others, Lionel Murphy, Doug McClelland and Barry Jones, with whom he shared an interest in American history.[66] In any event, few would – or could – pigeon-hole a man Menzies predicted "had better things ahead of him".[67]

4

MINISTERIAL CONSOLIDATION

Despite easy re-election at the 1951 Double Dissolution (where he was third on a joint Coalition ticket), and at the 1953 half-Senate election (where he was first), Gorton had to wait until after the 1958 House and half-Senate election before receiving Menzies' nod to enter the outer Ministry. By this time, the world view of a strong-willed Gorton appeared to have crystallised. But John Grey still lacked experience in the wielding of executive power.

Gorton's ministerial experience – the real training ground for any prime minister – appeared to consolidate both his style and substance: a predilection for "hands on" leadership; an eager breaking of convention to meet immediate needs; seeking advice outside conventional channels; unilateral decision-making; centralism over federalism; equality of opportunity; and an unwavering confidence both in himself and in an Australia buttressed by strong defence forces and well-resourced education facilities.

Navy

Menzies rewarded John Grey, not yet 50, with the Navy portfolio in 1958, largely because of the penetrating oratory skills that saw him labelled "chief baiter".[68] Gorton then began a ministerial career that wedded proactive management to an innate independence. For one, the new minister insisted his office be located within the Department of Navy building and not Parliament House as was the custom.

When Gorton found that even a modestly sized department could operate along frustratingly vertical lines of authority, he soon eschewed protocols and spoke directly with any public servant, regardless of rank, who held useful information. John Grey defended his approach in a military department: "the defence of Australia is best served by getting, in the quickest possible time, the greatest amount of the things that we need".[69] The new minister also demonstrated a strong work ethic, and some now spoke of him as a future leader. But his style remained informal, and he was often seen with "coat off, tie loosened [and] sometimes his braces hanging down".[70]

John Grey took to the Navy two traits that, as prime minister, would often work against him. The first was a relaxed and candid honesty that extended to the news media. To assist in his public relations, Gorton cultivated a close and fruitful relationship with Tony Eggleton, later Holt's press secretary and Liberal Party director.

A second continued to be Gorton's fiery temper – he was also obstinate and hated to be proved wrong – that too often resulted in bellicose responses to real or imagined affronts. Around this time, Gorton interpreted a comment from Labor Senator Don Willesee as an insult to wife Betty. While accounts vary, it appears Gorton and Willesee came to blows.[71] These were hardly the actions of a man hoping to lead Australia's most successful national party.

By the time he left the Navy in December, 1963, Gorton had upgraded offensive and defensive capabilities via significant capital investments. While Gorton did not win every budgetary battle, he signalled he could win most. Perhaps that was the root of Menzies' growing confidence when he invested in John Grey responsibility for steering a contentious *Matrimonial Clauses Bill* – designed to reform divorce law – through the Senate in 1959. Not only did Gorton easily execute its passage, he also flagged his own support for the marital rights of women: "[u]nder this bill the obligation of the husband to support the wife could more easily be enforced by the wife," Gorton said.[72]

John Grey also continued his anti-communist tirades and, in 1962, opposed demands for South Africa's expulsion from the British Commonwealth despite describing apartheid as "repugnant".[73] Gorton also resisted calls to relax a pernicious White Australia Policy, arguing in February, 1959, that

> above all, care should be taken to see that there does not develop in this country, as have developed in other countries, including Great Britain, colonies of people with a skin of different colour from that which we have. The Australian people can assimilate – and are assimilating – and can be friendly with many Asians who wish to come here and be citizens. But I fear that nothing would be more calculated to inculcate a colour consciousness, which Australia has not got, than for there to be in the cities of this country thousands or even tens of thousands of people of other nationalities living in little groups on their own…[74]

Today we can only condemn such parochialism, but it must remembered most Australians, including Labor leader Arthur Calwell, then endorsed racially determined immigration.

Education & Science

The Coalition's near-defeat at the 1961 election was a wake-up call for the Coalition. After having won by a single seat, Menzies knew he must undercut a resurgent Labor Party. That opportunity arrived in 1962 when New South Wales Labor Premier Bob Heffron pledged state funding for science laboratories in non-government schools. But Labor's Federal Executive – comprised of 36 non-parliamentary delegates ideologically opposed to private education – overrode the policy. This opened a pathway for Menzies to fund non-government schools directly from Canberra.[75] In addition to quietly advancing the Commonwealth's own power, Menzies could further wedge a Labor Party divided over private schools, emerge as a saviour for Roman Catholic voters, and again paint Labor as an organisation controlled by "36 faceless men".[76]

The impact of federal intervention in what had been jealously guarded state education policy was soon felt at a 1963 election also fought over a recovering economy and Labor's allegedly undemocratic internal policy-making processes. The fact the poll was held just a week after the assassination of U.S. President John F. Kennedy might also have proved critical, and it is therefore unsurprising the Coalition should be so easily returned with 10 additional seats.

With that election secured, Menzies – now almost 70 and unenthusiastic about fighting yet another campaign – pondered the Liberals' future. Given Gorton's successes in the Navy portfolio, it was inevitable Menzies should now promote John Grey and, in December, 1963, the now 52 year old assumed a new role: Minister in Charge of

Commonwealth Activities in Education and Research under the Prime Minister. The ambiguity of that title is well-based: while scientific research had been federally funded since 1916, the Commonwealth's role in state-based education remained constitutionally unclear in 1963. In short, there was no precedent for a stand-alone Commonwealth Minister for Education, and Gorton's portfolio was necessarily attached to the Prime Minister's office. Menzies also briefly appointed Gorton as Minister for the Interior (for just three months) and Minister for Works, a position he held till early 1967 and one that saw him sponsor a bill in 1966 to allow married women to work in the Commonwealth Public Service.[77]

In many ways, an education portfolio was the perfect fit for a man who long championed quality schooling as the path to equal opportunity. Moreover, Gorton, with Menzies' blessing, could flex some centralist muscle over the states and carve out a pioneering trail for Canberra. Indeed, Gorton in 1967 said that

> quite apart from the extensive interest which the Commonwealth has taken in tertiary education which has resulted in the revolutionising of such education, the Commonwealth in the secondary sphere has made very great contributions to the provision of scientific teaching aids in all secondary schools…[78]

It was an exciting time for education policy in Australia. Not only were the states enjoying Commonwealth grants for schools but, after the release of the 1964 *Martin Report* into higher education, the Commonwealth would now control a new generation of universities and colleges of advanced education. John Grey's tertiary education reforms thereafter included generously increased funding for both staff and infrastructure.

But Australian history could have been very different had one of Gorton's contemporaries spoken differently. In 1964, Menzies considered his Education Minister for the vacant position of Australian ambassador to Washington, and he sought an assessment from colleagues. When the conservative External Affairs Minister Garfield Barwick said Gorton was "rather headstrong", John Grey was ruled out.[79] Given his domestic ambitions, Gorton may well have refused the offer. In any case, John Grey was easily re-elected at the top of the ticket at the 1964 half-Senate election.

Menzies' retirement in January, 1966, was a turning point for a new generation of Liberals looking to emerge from their leader's long shadow. New Prime Minister Harold Holt was among them and, accordingly, retained Gorton in Education and Works. Following the Coalition's 1966 election landslide, Holt promoted John Grey to Cabinet as Minister for Education and Science. Holt's confidence was not misplaced: in his four years in the portfolio Gorton oversaw a 40 per cent increase in secondary school matriculations, and a 72 per cent increase in Commonwealth scholarships.[80] But, despite these successes, John Grey remained largely unknown outside political circles.

The year 1967 was a nadir for the Coalition. Holt was often bested in the House of Representatives by a reinvigorated Labor Party now led by an articulate Gough Whitlam, and the Liberals' large and restless backbench became increasingly critical of its leader. Worse, the Coalition was now fracturing as Federal Treasurer Billy McMahon – a free trade advocate – frequently clashed with protectionist Country Party leader Jack McEwen. Worse, McMahon was widely suspected to be a perpetual leaker – especially to the Packer press – of Cabinet deliberations. Indeed, Gorton told me in 1998 that McMahon worked against Holt "the whole time".[81] To bolster Government stocks in an increasingly troublesome Senate, Holt on 16 October promoted Gorton to Government Leader in that chamber. But the electorate had already decided: the Coalition lost two seats in a three per cent primary swing at the November, 1967, half-Senate election.

'VIP Affair'

A key factor in that swing was the so-called 'VIP Affair': a controversy long brewing over Government MPs' privileged use of RAAF aircraft. Labor, sensing a growing intolerance of politicians' perquisites, for months urged the Government to release the passenger lists Holt and Air Minister Peter Howson said did not exist.

An emboldened news media kept the saga alive before it came to a head immediately after Gorton's appointment as Government Leader in the Senate. Despite Gorton's best efforts, the furore continued, and a petulant Holt accused him of losing control of the Senate.[82] Coalition backbenchers became increasingly nervous, but the Prime Minister refused to budge. With the issue now consuming the Government, a determined Gorton, habituated to proactive decision-making, acquired and tabled the lists on 25 October. "Parliament is entitled to facts…which will enable members to form a judgment as to the purposes served by the flight and the manner in which it is being conducted," he told the Chamber.[83] John Gorton, Government Leader in the Senate for just nine days, had single-handedly defused an explosive political issue.

The effects were immediate and profound. First, the Liberals divided between those who admired Gorton's boldness and those who accused him of making Holt and Howson look duplicitous. After all, Gorton might have breached Cabinet confidentially. Either way, conservatives never forgave John Grey for what they saw as a betrayal.

Second, Gorton had demonstrated some sharp political instincts. The Education Minister knew the Government would only continue to haemorrhage should the documents not be produced and, by tabling the papers, Gorton muted Labor's attacks.

Most importantly, John Grey had emerged from political obscurity to become one of Australia's most recognisable faces. But this only further convinced Gorton's critics the Education Minister tabled the documents not to save the Government's fortunes but to enhance his own.

Leadership Transition

The Coalition was forced to consider leadership succession far sooner than it could have imagined. On a sweltering afternoon on Sunday, 17 December, 1967, a weary Harold Holt – enjoying a weekend break at Portsea, Victoria, after some of the most difficult weeks of his career – disappeared while swimming in boiling seas off Cheviot Beach. Despite lingering hope he would be found alive, senior figures knew a leadership transition must immediately commence.

Gorton's name was quickly proposed, as was McMahon's. The conservative Minister for External Affairs Paul Hasluck also nominated.

Gorton was clearly advantaged. First, in the days immediately after Holt's death, John Grey appeared widely on television and in the print media where his earthy nationalism and blokey athleticism were writ large. He also reassured middle Australia he was "slightly to the Left" among Liberals.[84] While conservatives were aghast, uncommitted colleagues were reassured by Gorton's easy ability to connect with both media and public. When, for example, a journalist asked Gorton about himself, John Grey light-heartedly replied, "I am six feet high and weigh about 12 stone".[85] That candour contrasted sharply with the reserved Hasluck who saw campaigning as gauche. Where Gorton was happy to canvass support even at Holt's funeral,[86] Hasluck relied only on his record.

But John Grey's most critical opportunity arrived when Country Party leader McEwen refused to serve in a Coalition led by McMahon who, to his credit, calmly stood aside. Australia's 19th prime minister would be decided from just four candidates: Gorton, Hasluck, the relatively junior Minister for Labour and National Service Les Bury, and the young Minister for Immigration Billy Snedden. McEwen would continue as caretaker prime minister until 9 January, 1968.

Interestingly, as Figure One reveals, a December, 1967, Gallup poll shows just how divided Australians were on the choice of their next prime minister.

Figure One

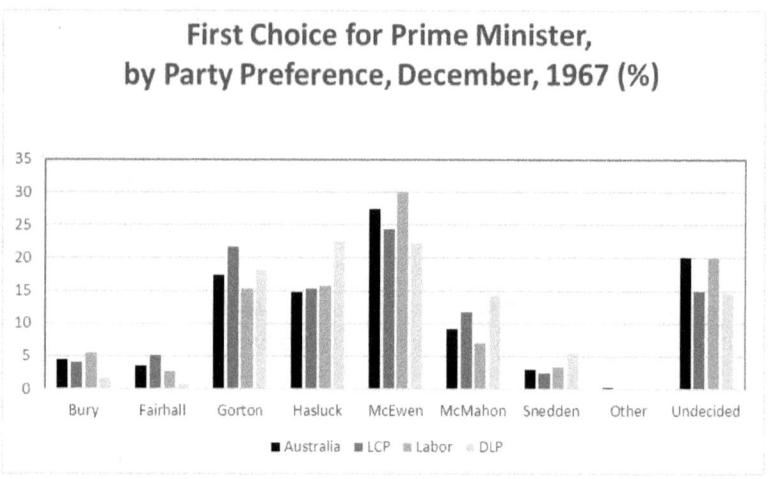

Source: *Morgan Gallup* Poll No. 195, 23 December, 1967.

It is interesting that one in four Australians hoped Country Party leader McEwen would continue as prime minister – an impossible option canvassed even among some Liberals. It is even more curious that Holt's logical successor, McMahon, should receive less than 10 per cent support overall, and that Hasluck – the candidate closest to the Menzian mould – should garner the support of fewer than one in seven. It is also critical that Gorton, after McEwen, was the first choice among Liberal voters, but only the second choice, behind the more conservative Hasluck, among Labor and DLP voters. This suggests liberals were eager for a political sea-change while conservatives were always resistant to Gorton.

Parties seldom reveal intra-party ballot results but the Liberals' second round tally – after Bury and Snedden had been eliminated on the first ballot from a party room of 81 – was reported to be convincing victory of 51 votes for Gorton and 30 for Hasluck.[87] As expected, John Grey enjoyed robust support from Senate colleagues. Gorton, sworn in as prime minister on 10 January, remained a Senator until 1 February – he would be the first prime minister since Edmund Barton to hold no seat in the House of Representatives – before contesting Holt's vacant seat of Higgins on 24 February. The fact he attracted a 6.1 per cent primary swing (despite a larger field) in Higgins suggests a new level of enthusiasm for a new type of Liberal leader, at least among a few leafy Melbourne suburbs.

Within the space of ten short weeks, John Grey had moved from junior Cabinet minister to Government Senate Leader to Liberal leader to the Prime Minister's office. In that time, Gorton had demonstrated the skills necessary to sew together disparate bases of support. The question now was how long he could keep that quilt from unravelling.

5

GORTON PM I:

IDEOLOGICAL LEADERSHIP

ANY deconstruction of Gorton's prime ministership necessarily invites a study of leadership more generally if we are to make assessments of prime ministerial success or failure.

'Transactional' and 'Transformational' Leadership

The eminent leadership scholar James Macgregor Burns divides leaders and leadership into two broad types. The first is the more common 'transactional' model: a compact between leader and followers which should "result in realizing individual goals of each".[88] For leaders, that goal will include earning the people's confidence long enough to win an election. For followers, it will include maintaining the core needs of employment, housing and public safety.[89] Burns's second type is the 'transformational': a model extending beyond short-term needs and toward a higher plane at which leaders "transform" society by "raising up" followers. Given 'transformational' leadership is primarily concerned with the "end-values" of liberty, justice and equality – and what Maslow identifies as the higher needs of "esteem" and "self-actualisation" (such as creative activities) – this form seeks the long-term goal of building a better society.[90] To this end, I argue Gorton attempted, but did not always deliver, 'transformational' leadership.

Leadership Context and Type

Political leaders should not be judged in a vacuum but instead assessed against the economic, social and cultural contexts in which they work. They should also be evaluated through the motivations of their followers – from close political subordinates to ordinary voters – who comprise half of any leadership equation.

To this end, Australian political scientist Graham Little explored three leadership contexts – where the leader's 'self' is juxtaposed against the 'other' – and the three leader types they produce. The first is the 'Structure' where leaders stand apart from followers to produce a traditionally 'Strong' leader atop a vertical hierarchy of authority.[91] In their propensity to defend the status quo, 'Strong' leaders are often 'transactional'. Robert Menzies is a prime example.

Little's second context is the 'Group' in which leaders are enmeshed with followers. This environment usually yields a consensual leader seeking co-operative decision-making along horizontal lines of communication.[92] This leader is also most often 'transactional', with Harold Holt a clear example.

A third is the 'Ensemble' in which leaders and followers establish a rapport under which "freedom and authority are reconciled".[93] This context can produce 'Inspiring' leaders who combine "purposefulness" with "consultation" and, thus, will lie somewhere between the 'Strong' and 'Group' types. Consequently, these leaders will operate across both vertical and horizontal lines of authority, with 'Inspiring' leaders often iconoclastic as they "resist ties that bind and rules that restrict". These leaders might also engage in "sheer exhibitionism" and, by operating "outside normal bounds", are likely to meet opposition when the "fluidity of their ideas" clashes with the "fixity of administration".[94] Given 'Inspiring' leaders verge on the apocryphal, Little argues this type is also the most likely to disappoint followers.[95] Accordingly, Gorton most strongly resembles the 'Inspiring' leader operating within an 'Ensemble' context.

Defining 'Gortonism'

The first step in exploring Gorton's paradoxical leadership is to unpack the man's political philosophy. While acknowledging that such adjectives as 'Deakinite' and 'Menzian' have long been used to describe certain prime ministerial traits, MacCullum notes Gorton was "the first of our prime ministers to become an abstract noun". As such, MacCullum defines 'Gortonism' as "centralism, almost socialism, even a form of iconoclasm which defied Liberal shibboleths and conventions".[96] Journalist Max Walsh in turn defined 'Gortonism' as

> a mixture of centralism in Commonwealth-State financial relations, isolationism in defence matters, populism and nationalism in fiscal matters [and] erraticism in government relations with business.[97]

By contrast, *The Financial Times* described 'Gortonism' as "a withdrawal from contact with other people's capital and policies, rather than an attempt to contribute something uniquely Australian".[98]

It is, of course, impossible to describe 'Gortonism' as a concrete ideology with clear philosophical boundaries: the fact the term is a journalistic invention rather than one of political science underscores its arbitrary nature. Moreover, Gorton – like so many political figures – appeared to be driven by policy action rather than philosophical reflection. And, like most leaders, Gorton and his world view suffered significant inconsistencies, and his policy delivery sometimes fell short of rhetorical promise.

In these contexts, Gorton was hardly unique. Perhaps that is why John Grey described 'Gortonism' to me simply as

> pushing forward all the time the capacity of Australia to make the most of the things it was producing and to spread them amongst the people of Australia as those things happened.[99]

This subtle reference to a form of redistribution of Australia's bounties would not be lost on Gorton's critics.

For the purposes of this book, I define 'Gortonism' as an amalgam of ideological and operational principles. In terms of the former, 'Gortonism' is a pragmatic application of an Australian economic and cultural nationalism that blended small 'l' liberal social policy with conservative tenets to produce a variegated liberalism that, in linking post-material values to the economically material, connected a conservative past to a liberal future. In terms of the latter, 'Gortonism' defines an operational leadership that champions quick action over lengthy reflection, administrative centralism over federalism, and prime ministerial over cabinet government.

The following section deconstructs the four elements – small 'l' liberalism, nationalism, centralism and 'owlish' foreign and defence policy, and their many sub-components – comprising 'Gortonism'.

Small 'l' Liberalism

Numerous observers identify an almost radical tradition in Gorton's prime ministership. Tiver, for example, argues Gorton's rhetoric was steeped in "Rooseveltian language", especially when John Grey insisted Liberals are not opposed to socialism in its "true sense".[100] Trengrove, too, describes Gorton as "a man trying not always very subtly to move his party to the left",[101] while Jupp claims Gorton's views were often "closer to those of Whitlam than to those of the conservatives in his own party".[102] This supports the view that Gorton served as a necessary ideological bridge between a conservative Menzies and a social democratic Whitlam.

Interestingly, many have read Gorton's commitment to welfare and education spending as evidence he had really been "a Labor man with socialist leanings" all along.[103] But Gorton was no Labor 'wolf' in Liberal clothing. Indeed, such conclusions ignore Gorton's life-long belief that Labor, despite Whitlam's post-1967 internal reforms, remained fundamentally "undemocratic".[104]

Instead, Gorton is best described as a "small 'l' liberal": a label he happily gave himself. But, critically, John Grey Gorton denied he was egalitarian, and insisted be believed foremost in "equality of opportunity".[105] This liberalism became manifest in commitments to policy reform in education, health and welfare, immigration, the environment, the arts, colonial independence, and in reforms for women, Indigenous Australians and, after leaving the prime ministership, in drug and abortion law reform and in rights for same-sex couples.

Public Education

As above, quality schooling for Gorton was not necessarily designed to create an equal Australia; it was to create an equality of opportunity for all Australians regardless of circumstance or geography. "There should be equivalents of standards in such things as education and health amongst all the areas of Australia, no matter in which area a citizen might live," Gorton said.[106] John Grey also boasted of his Government's $8 million allocation to the states for teacher training, and of his continuing support for senior secondary school scholarships.[107] As part of the *Nation-Wide Survey of Educational Needs*, the Prime Minister in 1970 also wrote to all state premiers demanding to know their schools' priorities. Importantly, college diploma courses were upgraded to degree status in 1968, and university enrolments during Gorton's prime ministership – from around 160,000 in 1968 to 200,000 in 1971 – far outstripped general population growth.[108]

Health and Welfare

A second element is found in Gorton's social welfare and health reforms. In addition to his establishment of a Social Welfare Unit within the Department of Prime Minister, John Grey said in 1969 that his Government "regard[ed] increasing the help given to poor families as of greater importance than abolishing a means test so pensions can be paid to rich families".[109] While pensions were initially means-tested under Holt in 1967, Gorton's new commitment raised conservative colleagues' ire, as did his 1970 pledge of a "war on poverty…to relieve the neglect and loneliness which some old people, who may not be poor, may now feel".[110] Indeed, Gorton was especially proud of his Government's delivery of a 15 per cent increase in age pensions.[111] John Grey, in collaboration with private medical insurers, also introduced health reforms which "removed the fear of expensive operations for Australians", with greater benefits for those with special needs or chronic illness.[112] Despite clashing with a medical profession insistent on higher charges, the Gorton Government over three years delivered free health care to 250,000 lower income families.

Yet, consistent with so many of Gorton's paradoxes, even his welfare policy retained conservative caveats: "My Government will review the field of social welfare with the object of assisting those in most need while at the same time not discouraging thrift, self-help and self-reliance," he said.[113]

Immigration and Indigenous Policy

A review of Gorton's immigration and Indigenous policies again reveal a blend of liberal and conservative tenets. He was, for example, a believer in 'Big Australia', and he oversaw an immigration program delivering around 450,000 migrants during his first two years in office. Yet Gorton also clung to the remnants of the White Australia Policy. In April, 1968, for example, Cabinet rejected a proposal from the moderate Snedden to admit migrants from Asia.[114] In that sense, Gorton was little different from Menzies or Holt.

This paradox extended to Gorton's policy on Indigenous Australians where the new Prime Minister "proved to be both an innovator and a conservative".[115] He was, for example, an ardent supporter of the 1967 referendum's 'Yes' campaign to allow the Commonwealth to legislate over Indigenous populations, and he was moved by a continuing lack of opportunity for an Aboriginal Australia plagued by poor health and entrenched poverty. The Prime Minister then oversaw in December, 1968, the granting of full wages to Aboriginal workers in the Northern Territory – a process begun in 1966 when the North Australian Workers' Union took a case to the Arbitration Commission which found in favour of extending award wages to Aboriginal pastoral workers. The *Aboriginal Enterprises (Assistance) Act* was also passed in 1968 and, the following year, the first Aboriginal Study Assistance Scheme provided for Aboriginal "advancement".[116] Gorton also appointed W.C. (Bill) Wentworth as the nation's first Minister for Aboriginal Affairs, and later pledged to override discriminatory state legislation.[117]

But Gorton also remained paternalistic toward Indigenous Australians whom, he insisted, must assimilate into white Australia. Moreover, Gorton's Cabinet in May, 1968, considered but shelved a land grant proposal for the Northern Territory Gurindji people at Wattie Creek.[118] Interestingly, it has been argued John Grey's paternalism was rooted in a latent Christian commitment derived from Christ's Sermon on the Mount: "Be ye therefore perfect as your Father in Heaven is perfect".[119] Even so, in the wake of the High Court's 1992 *Mabo* decision, Gorton insisted land rights were divisive and described Aborigines as "inferior" for a lack of agricultural practice.[120]

Women

Gorton's commitment to women's rights enjoys a prouder history. In early 1968, Cabinet approved "dollar for dollar" assistance for state governments to support "Deserted Wives…with Children".[121] Moreover, as early as 1962, Gorton supported "equal pay [for women] for equal work".[122] And while not originating with Gorton himself – the initial push for 'equal pay' began with unions in the Arbitration Commission, with four states legislating for wage equality by 1969 – the 'phasing in' of wage equity began during the first year of Gorton's prime ministership.

Arts

A fifth element of Gorton's liberalism is found in his commitment to the creative industries. In 1968, for example, John Grey brought the Australian Council for the Arts – established by Holt in 1967 – under his control in the Department of Prime Minister. He also increased the Council's funding by 75 per cent in his second year as prime minister.[123] Gorton also launched a National Film and Television Training School and, in 1970, an Australian Film Development Corporation that rebirthed Australian cinema. During debate on its establishment bill, Gorton again wedded pragmatism to idealism:

> …we expect profits in money terms but at least as importantly we expect profit in human values. A flourishing film industry in Australia will employ talented Australian writers, artists, directors, actors, musicians and technicians.[124]

Environment

Notably, in an age of rapid economic development when shopping centres were often prioritised above parks, Gorton flagged an early commitment to environmental conservation. Gorton roundly condemned, for example, Queensland's arch-conservative Bjelke-Petersen Government when it sought to mine the Great Barrier Reef, insisting

> the Barrier Reef, being one of the great wonders of the world, should not be in any way endangered and should not in any way run the risk of having its ecological balance disturbed, or in other ways put in jeopardy.... [the] drilling for oil is something which should not, as far as legal possibilities are concerned, take place.[125]

Nauru and Papua New Guinea

Gorton played a key role in the Holt Government's preparation for Nauru's independence from Australia in 1968, and later gave support to Papua New Guinea's independence. After Labor leader Gough Whitlam visited there, Gorton in July, 1970, made his own visit to Rabaul and received the hostile response he feared. In typical Gorton style, John Grey on that tour had secreted a pistol on his person and conceded he would have fired on any attackers.[126]

Same Sex Relationships

Gorton's liberal views on Gay law reform were aired only after he had left the prime ministership, but they nonetheless offer evidence of his evolving liberalism. In October 1973, Gorton moved in the House that "homosexual acts between consenting adults in private should not be subject to the criminal law". Gorton altruistically added that

> [t]his is one of those rare occasions – those all too rare occasions – when the Parliament can act as it was originally theoretically intended to act; that is, to act as a collection of men [sic], representing sections of the community, able to listen to a case and to make up their minds as to what is right without the constraints of party or of faction.[127]

Nationalism

Economic and cultural nationalism comprise a second pillar of 'Gortonism'. As explored above, while John Grey's proud Australianness manifested long before his accession to the prime ministership, it was only when independent of Menzies and Holt that Gorton fully realised a nationalism running to his 'bootheels'.

Economic Nationalism

First, it is interesting to note that, despite Australia's economic buoyancy, Gorton's Cabinet in 1968 rejected any increase in the minimum wage.[128] Instead, John Grey appeared more focused on the country's 'open door' foreign investment policies that many feared would see Australia become little more than a farm and quarry. Gorton, of course, had long championed an unashamedly nationalist economic position in which he claimed Australia could "buy back the farm". This included limiting foreign investment that, Gorton argued, had seen Australia adopt

> the posture of a puppy lying on its back with all legs

in the air and its stomach exposed saying, 'Please, please give us capital. Oh, tickle my tummy. Oh, on any conditions'.[129]

Perhaps the most widely cited example of Gorton's economic nationalism is his prevention, in late 1968, of a British takeover of the Australian-owned *MLC Insurance Company*. Despite Treasury's advice that the *British Sun Alliance Group* "could be trusted", Gorton believed Australians shared his suspicions. His economic nationalism was also evident in his development of an Australian oil pricing policy with *Esso-BHP* after the discovery of oil in Bass Strait,[130] and in his establishment of an *Australian Industry Development Corporation* designed to finance local industry.[131]

Gorton's hunch that Australians shared his economic nationalism was correct. A 1969 *Gallup* poll found, for example, that 79 per cent supported majority Australian ownership of Australian industry.[132] Yet, even here, Gorton's nationalism knew limits, especially in the face of criticism from the Liberals' free trade wing and from the private sector. Just weeks before the 1969 federal election, for example, Gorton insisted that

> a strong and continuing flow of overseas capital has never been questioned by [the] Government... The Government has, as its general objective, the encouragement of Australian participation in and partnership with overseas enterprises.[133]

In making a further break from a Britain that had already applied to join the European Economic Community, and flagged its intention to withdraw all military personnel from Southeast Asia, Gorton's Government in 1970 also committed Australia to metric conversion by 1980.

Cultural Nationalism

Gorton's cultural nationalism added another dimension, with the Prime Minister insisting that, on state occasions not involving the Monarch or Governor-General, *Waltzing Matilda* be played in lieu of *God Save the Queen*. But Gorton was not a republican, nor did he want to change the Australian flag.[134] Again, public opinion was on his side. In 1968, a Morgan Gallup poll found 75.7 per cent of Australians insisted it was more important to be regarded an Australian citizen than a British subject while, in 1969, 51.4 per cent favoured the replacement of *God Save The Queen* with an Australian anthem.[135] John Grey also saw the introduction of Australia's own *Copyright Act* designed to protect local intellectual property.[136]

There's even evidence of a military nationalism. Despite his relationship with U.S. President Richard Nixon being less warm than that between Holt and Lyndon Johnson, John Grey – locked into a 1963 contract to buy F-111 fighter aircraft from the United States – stood up to Nixon in 1970 and insisted on the right to reject delivery of the aircraft should they fail to meet Australian standards.[137]

Centralism

It is likely no single issue enraged Gorton's conservative critics more than his views on Commonwealth-State relations. Not only did John Grey argue the Australian economy should be managed "as a whole", he insisted on the federal government's superiority over the states in all areas, especially finance.[138] Indeed, Gorton wanted

> instead of six or seven small nations inside one

> nation, a people proud of the whole Australian nation and prepared to contribute to that one nation as well as to their own individual advancement.[139]

Amusingly, when asked if he was a Victorian, Gorton laconically replied, "buggered if I know".[140]

But, again, Gorton demonstrated internal contradictions when he argued in 1968 that he did not wish

> to interfere in [the States'] administration but would intervene if, for example, water conservation was being neglected in one of the six States and that State was falling behind the other States [to become] detrimental to Australia as a whole.[141]

In this sense, Gorton's model of federalism resembles a Deakinite liberalism that demanded national economic development for a collective national good. To this end, John Grey relied heavily upon the Commonwealth's special purpose grants, authorised by s.96 of the Australian Constitution, to steer the states' development. John Grey's centralism also extended to his desire for more control over state Liberal Party branches. In fact, Gorton conceded to me his admiration for Labor's internal structure that gave its national office power to intervene in state branches.[142]

Unsurprisingly, Gorton's centralism drew the antipathy of conservative state premiers Bob Askin (NSW) and Henry Bolte (Victoria). But Queensland's Joh Bjelke-Petersen reserved a special venom for Gorton when, in 1970, the Prime Minister quashed the Country Party Premier's demand to drill for oil on the Great Barrier Reef. During early debate on the *Territorial Sea and Continental Shelf Bill* in

1970, Gorton angrily asserted Commonwealth power over the states in controlling seabeds beyond a three-mile limit. Canberra's power, Gorton insisted, "was not an offer to the States...[it] was simply a clear and unequivocal statement of intention on the part of the Government".[143]

Ultimately, however, Gorton merely extended the centripetal federalism already practised by Menzies and Holt. But where Gorton's predecessors at least wrapped centralist tendencies in the diplomatic rhetoric of 'states' rights', John Grey appeared to relish the conflict with state premiers.

"Hawk", "Dove" and "Owl"

As outlined earlier, Gorton's "hawkish" anti-communism had been well established from his first days in the Senate. His rhetoric – undoubtedly rooted in personal belief but also used to electoral advantage – echoed Menzies' own, and that of a large minority of conservative Australians who, in 1951, had only narrowly lost a referendum to ban the Communist Party.[144] But, as anti-communism lost its currency in the late 1960s, Gorton adopted a more 'dovish' position and became, in his words, an 'owl': a term which expediently covers, under a mantle of supposed wisdom, a blend of liberal and conservative tenets. For example, while still avowedly anti-communist, Gorton now acknowledged a new global Left. The Czechoslovakian uprising in 1968, he now agreed, did not seek "to get rid of Communism but to keep Communism and have a measure of freedom too".[145]

Another example is found in 1967 when Gorton – still publicly supportive of the Vietnam War – now privately conceded he "was not so sure".[146] Moreover, John Grey, who had urged caution in sending combat troops to South Vietnam after 1964, openly opposed Holt's increased troop commitment in 1966, and rejected Nixon's unlimited bombing of North Vietnam after 1968.[147] By 1969, Gorton – who confirmed to me he thought "two [battalions] was more than enough"[148] – had flagged no replacement of the third battalion returning to Australia at year's end. Gorton also cut five per cent from the Defence budget to accommodate increased social welfare spending.[149]

But perhaps the clearest example of Gorton's increasingly liberal foreign policy is found in his approval of a speech given by External Affairs Minister Gordon Freeth in August, 1969. Freeth – addressing the presence of the Soviet Union in the Indian Ocean – said "Australia has to be watchful, but need not panic whenever a Russian appears".[150] The speech inevitably drew criticism from the arch-conservative DLP, and possibly cost Freeth his seat at the 1969 election.

Gorton now appeared to adopt the "Fortress Australia" doctrine of protecting Australia at home rather than abroad – although he insisted he was never such an advocate.[151] Either way, his Government now clearly rejected the 'Domino Theory' of transnational communist aggression and, in 1970, Australia signed the international Nuclear Non-Proliferation Treaty despite Cabinet concerns the agreement could weaken the United States' protective nuclear umbrella.[152]

But, again, 'hawkish' remnants remained in Gorton's foreign and defence policies. He refused, for example, to re-issue a passport to Australian journalist and communist sympathiser Wilfred Burchett, and he warned against any rapprochement with the People's Republic of China. Most memorably, Gorton – visiting Washington in June, 1969 – echoed the obsequiousness of Holt's 1966 "All the Way with LBJ" speech with an address reassuring Nixon that

> Australian support would be at hand wherever the United States is resisting aggression…wherever there is a joint attempt to improve, not only the material but the spiritual standards of life of the peoples of the world then, sir, we will go Waltzing Matilda with you.[153]

In sum, John Grey's ideological leadership appeared 'good' overall given 'Gortonism' brought real and enduring economic, administrative and cultural change. But, as the reforms were few, sometimes inconsistent and often poorly articulated, Gorton's ideological leadership fell short of 'great'. How Gorton's operational leadership fared is explored in the next chapter.

6

GORTON PM II: OPERATIONAL LEADERSHIP

Many in and beyond the Liberal Party room doubted Gorton's capacity to lead long before his accession to the prime ministership. But others believed the time was ripe for an audacious and plain-speaking leader. Hancock describes these divisions as "John the Bold" versus "Gorton the Unready".[154]

Interestingly, Gorton suggested to me that ambivalence to his leadership was rooted in his Senate origins, and that he was never really accepted by his House colleagues.[155] And while understanding these competing views offers insight into the already weakened party John Grey inherited from Holt, it also offers context for the fact Gorton served as prime minister during some politically challenging moments, including anti-war protest moratoria, the *Poseidon* nickel boom and bust, and a second Royal Commission into the 1964 HMAS Voyager tragedy that cost 82 lives.

Like evaluations of his legacy more generally, Gorton's operational leadership – his management of, and attitude toward, the prime ministership's day to day demands – has attracted enormous criticism. Liberal minister Hubert Opperman, for example, described Gorton's style as one littered with "contradictory statements and indifference to detail, disregard for punctuality [and] alien incoherency".[156] Air Minister Peter Howson similarly rated Gorton's parliamentary performances "woeful,"[157] while Minister and later Governor-General Paul Hasluck described John Grey as "ignorant of many practices, facts and conventions that are elementary in a constitutional democracy."[158]

Gorton critic Alan Reid also claimed John Grey had a "lack of intellectual preparation" for office, and that he was a

> deliberate experimenter, but indulged in experiments rather than planning them, like a carefree schoolboy mixing chemicals haphazardly for the excitement of seeing what would happen.[159]

Critically, Gorton conceded to me that, at least during the 1969 election campaign, he was at times "lackadaisical".[160]

As with the assessment of his ideological leadership in the previous chapter, Gorton's operational leadership must be explored through its constituent parts: erratic political communication, unilateral decision-making, and insouciant interpersonal relations. Importantly, any evaluation of that operational leadership must also consider how Gorton serviced the critical 'power points' – cabinet, backbench, the party's organisational wing, minor parties from which preferences are drawn, senior public servants, key pressure groups and the news media. This is required for any prime minister to maintain a coalescence of support. Importantly, as Reid argues, Gorton appears to have engaged only two 'power points': the Liberals' parliamentary wing and, through television, the Australian electorate at large.[161]

Erratic Political Communication

The first element is a mode of political communication best described as erratic, particularly when contrasted to the more coherent performances of the erudite Labor leader Gough Whitlam. Where Gorton's cavalier nonchalance and off-the-cuff comments initially proved appealing to voters looking for more relaxed and quintessentially Australian leader, that novelty was soon lost to Whitlam's consistently focused approach in both the Parliament and the news media.

As outlined above, most Australians became cognisant of Gorton via television during the 'VIP Affair' and immediately after Holt's death. Here, John Grey demonstrated a "genuine affection for people" that "showed no pretence and welcomed none".[162] But it is likely Gorton became over-reliant on television as a tool of political communication, and the new Prime Minister often chose it and not Parliament to make important policy announcements. Ironically, major announcements via televised media conferences is common practice today.

As noted earlier, Gorton was often lampooned for verbal *faux pas* and for allegedly mangling the English language. John Grey, for example, frequently addressed the House Speaker as "Mr President" and, while still an adroit parliamentarian, demonstrated the "wrong nuances – Senate nuances".[163] And, despite lively television appearances during his first year in office, Gorton's speeches in and beyond the House appeared to decline to the point of him becoming "a disturbingly uneven speaker".[164] In attempting to articulate the Coalition's health policy in 1969, for example, Gorton confounded his audience:

> The AMA agrees with, or I believe will agree with us, that is its policy, and it will be its policy, to inform patients who ask what the common fee is and what their own fee is so that a patient will know whether he is going to be operated on, if that's what it is, on

the basis of the common fee or not.[165]

Gorton also attracted criticism for his *Blair House* press conference during his first official visit, in April, 1968, to the United States. Here, Gorton failed to answer adequately a question of whether the defence of Malaysia and Singapore would be covered by the ANZUS agreement. After referring to 'Malaya' instead of 'Malaysia,' he unconvincingly insisted he chose his words purposely.[166] The core problem appeared to be Gorton's too often inadequate preparation for key moments, and an "unfortunate habit in thinking aloud about Australian foreign policy" to the point of "frequently contradicting himself".[167]

By contrast, others attest to Gorton's powerful engagement with live audiences where his speeches often received a "rapturous reception".[168] Even Alan Reid conceded Gorton "was not devoid of talent at handling a mass meeting".[169]

As above, a key criticism of Gorton's operational leadership has been his cultivation of a Liberal Party backbench at the expense of Cabinet. But even junior members of the Government often felt excluded from the Prime Minister's political communication. Consequently, Liberals Fred Chaney, Jim Killen, Don Chipp, Andrew Peacock and others formed the "Mushroom Club": an informal dining group, with ties emblazoned with fungi, who felt they had been "kept in the dark and fed bullshit". In typical Gorton style, the self-effacing John Grey insisted on joining and, when he did, was ordained 'Chief Spore'.[170]

Gorton's initially healthy relationship with the news media also deteriorated. While Holt held media conferences weekly, Gorton allowed this practice to lapse and – despite privately briefing favoured journalists in his office[171] – he now appeared "aloof".[172] John Grey could also be frustratingly cryptic with the press. On his return from a visit to the United Kingdom in 1969, for example, Gorton peevishly replied to a journalist's question on the success of his trip: "The catering was excellent at Buckingham Palace and the soup was hot," he snapped.[173]

A pivotal moment arrived in late 1968 when John Grey refused to quell speculation of an early election. Damagingly, the subsequent anticlimax of no election frustrated a Fourth Estate, and even his most loyal followers. By the time Gorton described journalists as "slimy white things that crawl out of sewers", it was clear his relationship with them had soured.[174] Such acrimony could only have sharpened journalists' instincts when reporting the personal indiscretions described below.

Unilateral Decision-Making

Gorton carried into his prime ministership a penchant for making decisions quickly and often without consultation. It was said, for example, that John Grey would conceive policy in the bath in the morning and present it to Cabinet as a *fait accompli* before lunch.[175]

Indeed, just days after assuming the top job, John Grey said

> the Prime Minister, now or in the future, is not to be Chairman of the committee so that a majority vote in the committee says what's going to be done. He should put to the Cabinet or the committee what he believes ought to be done, and if he believes strongly

enough that it ought to be done, then it must be done.[176]

Indeed, Gorton confirmed to me he rejected the Westminster convention of *primus inter pares* – 'first among equals' – that positioned a prime minister as no more important than his or her cabinet colleagues. Prime ministers are "expected to lead or get out," he said.[177] In one sense, this appears a mere amplification of Menzies' practice (eschewed by Holt) of dominating cabinet through the sheer force of personality.[178] Nonetheless, Gorton's unilateral decision-making remains a watershed in the evolution of Australian government from 'cabinet' to 'prime ministerial.'

As outlined earlier, one example of Gorton's unilateralism is his prevention in 1968 of a British take-over of the Australian-owned *MLC Insurance Company*. Here, John Grey ignored official advice and trusted – rightly, it seems – his own judgement that Australians shared his economic nationalism. A second lies in Gorton's personal negotiations with *Esso-BHP* to establish a new oil pricing policy – a delicate procedure almost certainly requiring economists' expertise. But perhaps the most widely cited is Gorton's statement not to increase Australia's military commitment to Vietnam following the January, 1968, Tet Offensive that now pointed to an unwinnable war for the West. But, on this occasion, Gorton did not make new policy 'off-the-cuff' but merely reiterated a decision already taken by Holt.[179]

This preference for autonomy also arguably manifested in Gorton's adoption of Menzies' practice of dispatching political rivals to plum postings[180] when John Grey appointed Paul Hasluck in early 1969 as Australia's 17th Governor-General. It was also demonstrated in his immediate splitting of the Department of Prime Minister and Cabinet into a stand-alone Department of Cabinet, headed by John Bunting (a "stick-in-the-mud conservative", Gorton said)[181], and a stand-alone Department of Prime Minister headed by Gorton's friend, Lenox Hewitt.[182] In splitting the department, Gorton might have gained sovereignty in policy-making, but he also separated himself from politically sensitive 'power points'.

Gorton's Cabinet process further underscored this separation. In addition to what appeared to be an overtly 'presidential' style, John Grey also ignored the longstanding convention of circulating Cabinet papers one week prior to meetings. By also allowing Cabinet's powerful Foreign Affairs and Defence Committee to fall into disuse, John Grey further weakened his links across the Party.[183] Even more worryingly, Gorton cultivated an after-hours 'cocktail cabinet' where he met favoured ministers to discuss policy over drinks.[184] This can only have further wedged an already divided frontbench.

But several contemporaries reject claims of John Grey's unilateralism. Navy Minister Jim Killen, for example, told me Gorton "in no way" behaved liked a president and, moreover, punctiliously observed Westminster convention in ensuring Attorney-General Tom Hughes attended meetings to clarify legal points. Ministers were also encouraged to air even the most unpopular opinions.[185] Gorton also approximated Menzies' Cabinet meeting schedule of around 70 per year.[186]

Ultimately, the late-rising John Grey – who was often late to critical meetings after chatting informally with groups visiting parliament[187] – was criticised as a "Monday to Friday" prime minister.[188] Despite this, Gorton maintained supreme confidence in himself: "I am always prepared to recognize that there can be two points of view – mine, and the one that is probably wrong".[189]

Insouciant Interpersonal Relations

Gorton's nonchalance in his private and public lives was clearly evident. As explored in Chapter Two, that insouciance was likely shaped by Gorton's war-time experiences, and underscored by an insistence on a private life despite being Australia's most recognisable political figure. Gorton's ministers recount, for example, how John Grey would elude his night security team – by jumping over the back fence of The Lodge or hiding in the back of his ministerial limousine – to attend local parties.[190] It was also manifest in a comment made to Gorton by Queensland DLP Senator Gair before John Grey's visit to Washington. "Behave yourself," Gair demanded. Gorton replied with predictable vigour: "John Grey Gorton will bloody well behave precisely as John Grey Gorton bloody well decides he wants to behave".[191]

Once again, contradictions are found within Gorton's interpersonal relations. Where Country Party leader Doug Anthony told me he found Gorton "direct in attitudes,"[192] Hasluck described John Grey as "affectionate and sentimental" but, also, a man who "treat[ed] too many people as fools or knaves and trie[d] to brush them aside."[193] And while St John admired Gorton's "philosophy of mateship,"[194] he concluded that Gorton's "impression of charm and sweetness…belie[d] the true arrogance of his nature".[195] Labor speechwriter Graham Freudenberg similarly claimed Gorton was "given to slow anger and lasting grudges," and that he was "a man of the vendetta"[196] – a summation Labor's Dr Jim Cairns echoed to me in 2000.[197]

Above all, Gorton insisted on a casualness at every level of his prime ministership. In early 1971, for example, he commissioned artist June Mendoza to paint his official portrait, but refused to pose in a conventional suit. John Grey instead wore a suede jacket and cravat, and his remains the only prime ministerial portrait in King's Hall, Parliament House, not featuring its male subject with a tie.

This insouciance was also manifest in Gorton's relationship with alcohol which, Gorton conceded, he over-used.[198] Worse, John Grey, unlike Labor leader Bob Hawke, made no attempt to address his drinking on coming to the top job. Indeed, it was not uncommon for Gorton to appear inebriated – Mungo MacCallum regularly wrote of John Grey's "lubricated public appearances"[199] – with the Prime Minister's subsequent absences put down to "Gorton 'flu".[200] Perhaps the most telling anecdote comes from a cabin crew member who, on a prime ministerial flight, cleaned up after John Grey had been ill. "I suppose you're surprised that an old RAAF man like me can still get airsick," Gorton said apologetically. "I am actually, Prime Minister," the crew member replied, "because the plane hasn't taken off yet".[201]

But it was Gorton's preference for the company of women that both aggravated his critics and provided the juiciest media copy. The most widely cited example of Gorton's close relationship with a woman outside his marriage is his appointment, to the powerful position of Principal Private Secretary to the Prime Minister, of the 22 year old Ainsley Gotto: an attractive and arguably unqualified person who appeared to exert "undue influence" over John Grey (a charge Gorton denied) in acting as 'gate-keeper' to the Prime Minister's office from which senior ministers, and even wife Bettina, could be denied entry. Ministers also resented Gotto's informality – she addressed all by their first names – and an attitude critics claimed was "abrupt, rude and disrespectful". Indeed, when Dudley Erwin was asked the reason for his removal from Cabinet after the 1969 election, he replied, "It wiggles, it's shapely…and its name is Ainsley Gotto".[202]

The most damaging element to the Gorton-Gotto relationship, however, was the inevitable rumour of a sexual liaison. But Ian Hancock, biographer of both Gorton and Gotto, found no evidence of an affair, and we can only conclude the rumour was baseless. Indeed, Gotto was in a relationship with Opposition leader Gough Whitlam's own Principal Private Secretary, Race Mathews[203] - a potential conflict of interest in some ways far more scandalous. Years later, however, Gorton confirmed to Hancock he had indeed engaged in extra-marital affairs.[204]

Gorton met innuendo regarding two other women. The first, of lesser consequence, involved American cabaret singer Liza Minnelli who, in March, 1969, performed at the *Chequers* night club in Sydney. Given Minnelli's high profile as the attractive young daughter of Judy Garland, it is little wonder Gorton's post-show visit to her dressing room sparked gossip. But the fact Gorton and Minnelli were never alone was clearly lost on critics.[205]

A second and far more damaging incident involved 19 year old journalist Geraldine Willesee, daughter of Labor Senator Don Willesee. After a press gallery dinner on 1

November 1968 – as U.S. President Johnson announced a halt to the bombing of North Vietnam – Geraldine rode in Gorton's car. More worrying was the fact Gorton, who had been invited to call on U.S. Ambassador William Crook to discuss recent developments, took the uninvited Geraldine to the American Embassy after midnight. Worse, Gorton appeared to be more interested in talking with Geraldine than with Crook and, later, indiscreetly shared with the journalist his desire to withdraw all troops from South Vietnam.[206]

The following March, Labor MP Bert James – quoting Franke Browne's salacious newsletter *Things I Hear* – raised the matter in the House. When Max Newton's *Insight* also published rumours (later covered in the mainstream press) the puritanical Edward St John fired up his opposition to Gorton. The fact accounts varied as to whether Geraldine requested or Gorton offered the ride punctured the Prime Minister's reputation for honesty, and undoubtedly forced at least some voters, once enamoured with his larrikinism, to re-assess their support for the prime minister.

Public Opinion

No evaluation of Gorton's leadership would be complete without an analysis of how voters themselves rated it. Given the poor light many historians have painted his prime ministership, it is perhaps counter-intuitive to discover – as detailed in Figure Two, below – that John Grey maintained strong personal public approval until the second half of 1969. Only in August – some 20 months into his term – did Gorton's approval dip below 60 per cent, and only in the days before the October election did it fall below 50, with a slight recovery on election eve. Critically, Gorton's approval ratings always exceeded his disapproval: a phenomenon less commonly found today. Indeed, even at his nadir, Gorton saw fewer than one third of Australian voters disapprove of his leadership.

Figure Two

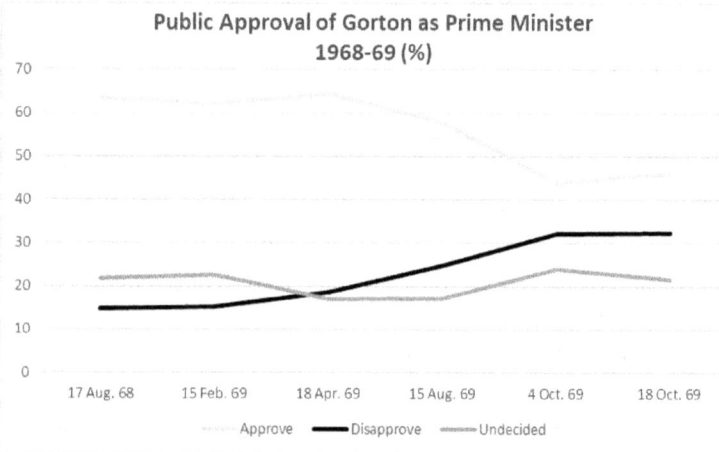

Source: *Morgan Gallup* Polls Nos. 193, 202-207.

Figure Three, below, indicates just how severely the 'VIP Affair' and other issues had wounded the Holt Government. While the last poll before Holt's death saw the Coalition still leading Labor, the Gorton Government's loss of seven points in primary vote support since the election just 12 months prior now panicked Government members. But, the fact Gorton had lost no more support by October 1969, than Holt had already lost in 1967 clearly undermines any claim of Gorton as sole or principal architect of the

Coalition's near-defeat at the 1969 election. Instead, with Government support spiking above 50 per cent in February 1968, it is clear voters were genuinely enamoured with their new Prime Minister. It seems Whitlam was right to call Gorton a "formidable opponent".[207]

Figure Three

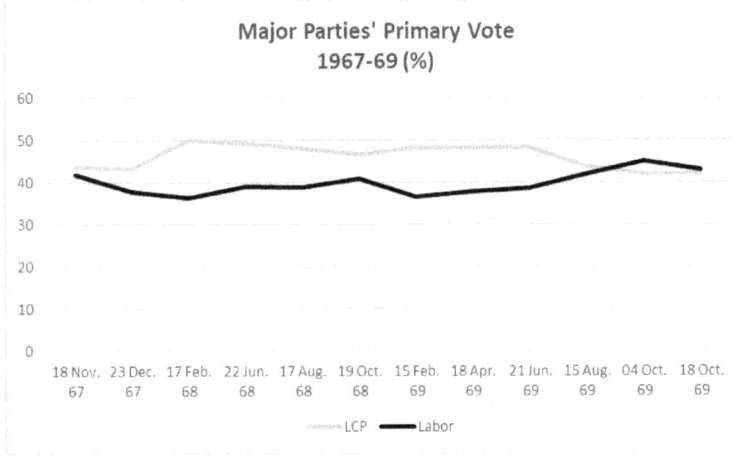

Source: *Morgan Gallup* Polls Nos. 194-207.

Critically, the Coalition's primary vote remained above 45 per cent until late 1969, and fell only marginally behind Labor's on election eve. But events other than Gorton's alleged indiscretions contributed to that movement between June and October. In July, for example, Labor convened an expanded federal conference – covered favourably by the news media – which now included Whitlam and other parliamentary leaders. The period also saw the DLP attack the Gorton Government over Freeth's speech, and some former Liberal moderates – already splitting in 1966 to form the Liberal Reform Group – launch the Australia Party as an ideologically centrist alternative. That party attained a respectable 17.5 per cent vote at the 1970 Australian Capital Territory by-election.

The above points to a critical conclusion: Gorton's operational leadership can only be rated as 'poor' after he disrupted his own 'Ensemble' by failing to service the many 'power points' buttressing a prime ministership. As explored in the next chapter, this disruption ensured his political demise.

7

THE GOING OF GORTON

The Coalition's loss of 16 seats (15 from the Liberals alone) to Labor made a Liberal Party leadership challenge inevitable in late 1969. On 2 November, National Development Minister David Fairbairn declared his hand, as did deputy leader McMahon after Country Party leader McEwen lifted his previous veto. On 7 November, Gorton was re-elected on the first ballot, with up to 45 votes from a 65-strong party room. McMahon was re-elected deputy leader against Snedden and Alan Hulme.[208]

Figure Four, below, reveals how support for the Coalition continued to decline throughout 1970, with Labor's primary vote overtaking the Coalition in the second half of that year.

Figure Four

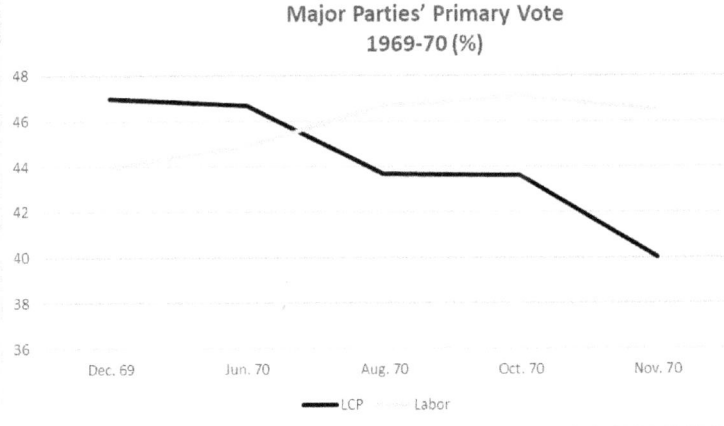

Source: *Morgan Gallup* polls; *Australian Political Facts*, (eds) Ian McAllister, Malcolm Mackerras, Alvaro Ascui and Susan Moss, Longman Cheshire, Melbourne, 1990, pp. 93-94.

Moreover, Labor leader Gough Whitlam bested John Grey in the only two polls to measure leadership approval in 1970. While Whitlam led Gorton in June, 49.0 to 46.0, that gap had narrowed by October, 45.2 to 44.1 per cent.[209]

But a more electorally competitive Gorton did little to quiet those intent on forcing change. The catalyst for that change arrived in March, 1971, when Defence Minister Malcolm Fraser resigned from Cabinet after alleging a lack of support from Gorton during a relatively minor dispute with Defence Chief of Staff, and Gorton friend, General Thomas Daly. During subsequent debate in the House (in which Fraser said Gorton was "not fit to hold the great office of prime minister"), prominent journalist Alan Ramsey screamed "You liar!" from the press gallery as the Prime Minister relayed his version of events. In typical Gorton style, John Grey later accepted the journalist's apology and urged Labor to drop its parliamentary censure of Ramsey.[210]

Under pressure, Gorton had no choice but to call a party room meeting for 10 March. Here, John Grey's usually sharp political acumen appeared to abandon him: had Gorton, as Chairperson, called for a motion of 'no confidence' in his leadership and not one of 'confidence,' opposition might have been more difficult to marshal. In any event, Gorton eschewed a show of hands for a secret ballot, and the 66 MPs divided 33-all. Interestingly, had the absent Herbert MP and Gorton ally Bob 'Duke' Bonnet been present, John Grey could have survived. But, in the end, Gorton ignored calls for a new ballot and gave a second (casting) vote against himself: a tie is not an expression of confidence, he said. Again in typical Gorton style, John Grey broke party rules: chairpersons do not enjoy both a deliberative and casting vote. Gorton then nominated McMahon who easily won a ballot against Snedden. Again paradoxically, Gorton nominated for the deputy leadership and won against Fraser and Fairbairn.

Figure Five, below, confirms that McMahon – despite a minor recovery in late 1972 – could not reverse the Coalition's downward spiral, nor his approval own rating that now fell below 30 per cent. Such a poor reception is perhaps unsurprising: McMahon, in attempting to steer the Liberals back to a Menzian past, might have placated the Party's conservative wing, but he did little to court an increasingly liberal Australia that, among other developments, saw the launch of the Australian Women's Lobby in early 1972.

McMahon, for example, resisted calls for universal health care and, when Gough Whitlam visited China in 1971, he ridiculed the Opposition leader before he, himself, was humiliated by U.S. President Richard Nixon's announcement of his own China visit. McMahon's only genuinely liberal innovation came in August, 1971, when he announced a phased withdrawal of Australian combat troops from South Vietnam.[211] The last battalion returned to Sydney in December, 1971, with Labor Prime Minister Whitlam recalling the last military advisers in December, 1972, and the last embassy guards in July, 1973.

Interestingly, given the relatively modest 2.5 per cent 2PP swing against the Coalition in 1972, there has long been speculation that Gorton, a man enjoying higher and longer public approval than McMahon, might have kept the Whitlam juggernaut at bay.

Figure Five

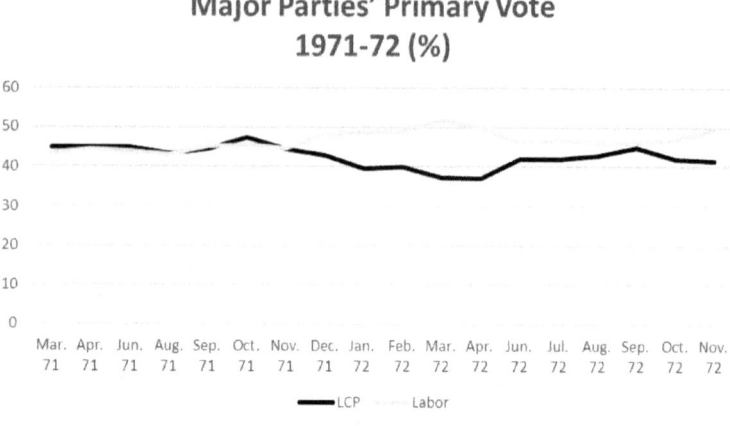

Source: *Morgan Gallup* polls; *Australian Political Facts*, (eds) Ian McAllister, Malcolm Mackerras, Alvaro Ascui and Susan Moss, Longman Cheshire, Melbourne, 1990, pp. 93-94.

As outlined earlier, Gorton wrote a series of acerbic articles for the *Sunday Australian* newspaper between August and September, 1971, in which he defended his prime ministerial style and imprudently rebuked conservative colleagues.[212] By August, 1971, McMahon had no choice but to dismiss Gorton from the frontbench.

John Grey was nonetheless re-elected to Higgins in 1972 despite suffering a primary swing about twice – and a 2PP swing almost three times – the national average. New Opposition leader Snedden then re-appointed Gorton to the frontbench as environment spokesman. Interestingly, Gorton later admitted he was asked at this time to establish a new centrist party.[213] Ignoring the plea, John Grey continued to move to the ideological left and, in 1973, moved a motion for Gay law reform (a politically hollow gesture given the states' jurisdiction over the issue) that easily passed the House under a conscience vote, 64 to 44.[214] He also campaigned for abortion law reform. But John Grey's continuing leftward trajectory in social policy must be seen in context: advocacy after leaving the prime ministership is very different from that while in the top job.

John Grey was re-elected to Higgins at the 1974 Double Dissolution, this time with a primary swing slightly above – and a 2PP swing more than double – the national mean. Despite his natural affinity with Gorton, Snedden in late 1974 removed John Grey from his shadow cabinet and, the following March, the now 63 year old Gorton declared he would retire at the following election. When Snedden's leadership failed to win the confidence of either voters or the Liberal backbench, Fraser on 21 March 1975, replaced him as Party leader. A disgusted Gorton walked out of the Liberal Party room and never returned. He officially resigned his Liberal membership on 23 May 1975.

Gorton thereafter became a voluble critic of Fraser – he described the new leader as a "disaster" and "extreme right wing"[215] – and publicly opposed Fraser's tactic of blocking Labor's Supply bills in the Senate in late 1975. Indeed, Gorton had long argued no Upper House should possess the power to withhold Supply.[216] John Grey then campaigned as an independent Senate candidate for the Australian Capital Territory, and urged supporters to vote Labor in the House of Representatives. Gorton attracted almost 12 per cent of the vote.

Paradoxically, John Grey now enjoyed something of a resurgence in his popular appeal, including among young Australians. In 1975, he appeared on Norman Gunston's television comedy – where he engaged actor Garry McDonald in a self-effacing manner – and in a promotional advertisement for the ABC's youth music program *Countdown*. Gorton between 1977 and 1981 also enjoyed a new career as a radio commentator where advocated the decriminalisation of prostitution and drugs – governments should dispense heroin to addicts, he said – and flagged his desire to end "union bashing" and media monopolies.[217] Loosening his previous support for an Australian monoculture, Gorton also urged Australians to embrace Vietnamese refugees. Immediately after the March, 1983, federal election, John Grey congratulated the Labor Prime Minister Bob Hawke for "rolling that bastard Fraser".[218]

Bettina Gorton died in 1983 and, a decade later, John Grey married Nancy Home and lived the remainder of his days in Vaucluse, Sydney. The Right Honourable John Grey Gorton – appointed Privy Councillor in 1968 and a Companion of Honour in 1971 – was knighted GCMG in 1977, appointed a Companion of the Order of Australia in 1988, and received a Centenary Medal in 2001. John Grey made his last public appearance in March, 2002, and he died just weeks later on 19 May. Covered widely by the news media, the end of a paradoxical life was nostalgically recalled by friends and foes alike.

He is buried at Melbourne General Cemetery.

8

"GO OUT IN VARIOUS DIRECTIONS":

THE LEGACY OF A PARADOXICAL PRIME MINISTER

This book has analysed John Gorton's leadership along two axes: the ideological and the operational. On each axis, Gorton broke new ground of his own while continuing the reforms of his predecessors.

In terms of the ideological, Gorton attempted genuinely 'transformational' leadership – and distinguished himself from prime ministers before him – by significantly increasing the age pension, rebooting the Australian film industry, and establishing Australia's first Commonwealth Aboriginal Affairs Minister. John Grey also pioneered national environmental protection, reversed a number of Australian foreign and defence policies – especially regarding an alleged communist 'threat' and Australia's military commitment to the Vietnam War – and cultivated an Australian economic and cultural nationalism.

But Gorton also found success in continuing the reforms of his predecessors, including heavy investment in the arts and public education, means-testing age pensions, overseeing a large migration program, continuing the momentum to bring independence to Nauru and Papua New Guinea, and in accelerating the pragmatic federalism of Menzies and Holt.

In terms of the operational, Gorton attempted

'transformational' leadership in his political communication by pioneering the use of television, and in his management of cabinet where, in prioritising unilateral decision-making, John Grey distinguished himself from predecessors via a 'prime ministerial' approach to cabinet government not uncommon today.

Because none of these reforms came without controversy and, because the Liberal-Country Party Coalition suffered a mammoth swing at the 1969 federal election, many concluded the Gorton "experiment" had failed. But did it?

Most political leaders demonstrate personal complexities and, at one time or another, reveal questionable – even paradoxical – behaviours in their public or private lives. The long and exasperating ascent up the political 'greasy pole' would simply prove too senseless for those who did not.

Even so, John Grey Gorton appeared especially possessed of complexities. Drawing evidence from the circumstances of his birth and childhood, from his education and wartime experiences, and from his relationships with women and alcohol, we can assume Gorton was probably the most complex and paradoxical individual to hold Australia's highest public office.

This book unpacked these complexities via three questions: are popular Australian histories, like Reid's, correct in painting Gorton's prime ministership in such poor light? How has 'Gortonism' shaped Australian liberal thought and practice? And does Gorton's operational leadership, while clearly unconventional, offer any lessons today?

We can draw four conclusions from the above. First,

many historians have been myopic in describing Gorton's prime ministership as 'poor' overall, and even more so in apportioning overwhelming blame to him for the Coalition's near-defeat in 1969. The power of an invigorated news media, the demands of a younger and increasingly diverse electorate, the distraction of a conservative bloc at war with itself, the impact of global political change, and the appeal of a resurgent Labor Party and its charismatic leader also eroded the Liberals' vote.

A second is that John Grey's operational leadership fell well short of that required of a 'great' or even a 'good' prime minister. While theorists might describe Gorton as 'Inspiring' in his ideological leadership, John Grey's erratic political communication, his penchant for unilateral decision-making and his insouciant interpersonal relations all point to 'poor' operational leadership. Indeed, in servicing too few 'power points', John Grey's iconoclasm so disrupted the political 'Ensemble' that effective operational leadership became almost impossible. Like so many 'Inspiring' leaders, Gorton ultimately disappointed many followers, and that dissatisfaction contributed to the Coalition's poor 1969 result.

Third, we can conclude that Gorton found real, if limited, success in an attempt at 'transformational' leadership comprised of his own pioneering reforms, and in those he continued from his predecessors. In that context, Gorton's ideological leadership can be described as 'good', but its inherent inconsistencies and limited composition saw it fall short of 'great'.

A final conclusion is that Gorton's prime ministership, while of a 'mediocre' or 'lower average' standard overall, was not an inert 'place-holder' between Menzies and Whitlam. Instead, Gorton's leadership between 1968 and 1971 – in conjunction with Holt's (1966-67) before it – served as an important cultural bridge connecting a conservative British past to a liberal Australian future. Ultimately, John Grey saw himself as a prime minister "of the times". Indeed, Gorton said that, by the late 1960s,

> we had reached a stage where we were on top of a mountain and we had to decide whether we stayed up there or go out in various directions and I remember distinctly thinking that at the time we looked at everything and saw how we could improve…[219]

Satisfyingly for Gorton, Whitlam – after McMahon's largely torpid prime ministership – accelerated the rate of reform under his own government between 1972 and 1975. These developments – universal health care, a final withdrawal from South Vietnam, an expansion of social welfare and education (including university) services, wage justice for women, social justice for Indigenous and migrant Australians (including the final abolition of the White Australia Policy), environmental protection, increased investment in the arts, independence for Papua New Guinea, and replacing *God Save the Queen* with *Advance Australia Fair*[220] – owed much to the groundwork Gorton and Holt had laid.

So, was the Gorton "experiment" a failure? Ultimately, no. Even Gorton's fiercest critics would concede that John Grey brought a fearless determination to an increasingly moribund LCP Government then coasting under the inertia of 18 years' incumbency. Indeed, Gorton soon injected an authentic nationalism and a reformist zeal – genuinely 'transformational' qualities – where there had previously been only the 'transactional' politics of short-term electoral survival.

And that points to one final conclusion: frustrated with a 'risk-averse' leaders hemmed in by opinion polls, focus groups and public relations 'spin', Australians looking for a genuineness in their political leaders would today very likely welcome another quintessentially Australian John Grey Gorton.

Notes

1. John Gorton, *Meet the Press*. Transcript No. 1764. 21 January, 1968. https://pmtranscripts.pmc.gov.au/release/transcript-1764
2. Mungo MacCallum, "A Larrikin in the Lodge", *Sydney Morning Herald, (Spectrum)*, 16 March, 2002, p. 8.
3. Colin Hughes, "Australian Political Chronicle, The Commonwealth: September-December 1969," *Australian Journal of Politics and History*, Vol. 16, No. 1, 1970, p. 74.
4. Judith Brett, *Australian Liberals and the Moral Middle Class*, Cambridge University Press, Melbourne, 2003, p. 142.
5. Norm Abjorensen, "Australia's Top 10 PMs," *The Canberra Times*, 5 December, 1992, Section C, p. 1.
6. Tony Walker and Jason Koutsoukis, "The good, the bad and the couldabeens," *Australian Financial Review*, 3 January, 2001, p. 28.
7. Michael Gordon and Michelle Grattan, "Curtin: Our greatest PM," *Age*, 18 December, 2004, p. 1.
8. Paul Strangio, *"Evaluating Prime-Ministerial Performance: The Australian Experience"*, in Paul Strangio, Paul 't Hart and James Walter, (eds), *Understanding Prime-Ministerial Performance: Comparative Perspectives*, Oxford University Press, Oxford, 2013.
9. Malcolm Mackerass, "Ranking Australia's prime ministers," *Sydney Morning Herald*, 25 June, 2010. https://www.smh.com.au/national/ranking-australias-prime-ministers-20100624-z3bn.html
10. John Gorton, "Liberal Party: Attitudes and Policies," in Henry Mayer, (ed), *Australian Politics: A Second Reader*, Cheshire, Melbourne, 1969; John Gorton, "The role of the PM," in Henry Mayer, (ed), *Australian Politics: A Second Reader*, Cheshire, Melbourne, [1968] 1969; John Gorton, "Australian Federalism: A View from Canberra," in Allen Patience and Jeffrey Scott, (eds), *Australian Federalism: Future Tense*, Oxford University Press, Melbourne, 1983.
11. Alan Trengrove, *John Grey Gorton: An Informal Bibliography*, Cassell, Melbourne, 1969.
12. Alan Reid, *The Gorton Experiment*, Shakespeare Head, Sydney, 1971.
13. Edward St John, *A Time to Speak*, Sun Books, Melbourne, 1969, p. 274.
14. *The Bulletin*, 1 November 1969, p. 19.
15. Personal communication with the author, 1998.
16. Reid, *The Gorton Experiment*, p. 21.

17 John Howard, *The Menzies Era: The Years that Shaped Modern Australia*, Harper Collins, Sydney, 2014, p. 494-96.
18 Personal communication with the author, 1998.
19 John Cramer, *Pioneers, Politics and People*, Allen and Unwin, Sydney, 1989, pp. 198-202.
20 Personal communication with the author, 2000.
21 Gervais Greene, "His own adventure," *Sunday Age*, 4 June, 1995, p. 5.
22 A. J. P. Taylor, *From Napoleon to Stalin*, Right Book Club, London, 1950.
23 Nikolai Bukharin, *Historical Materialism: A System of Sociology* [1926], Routledge, Oxford, 2011.
24 Paul Williams, "A Liberal Decline: An Analysis of the Electoral Decline of the Liberal Party, 1966-69," Unpublished Ph.D. thesis, University of Queensland, St. Lucia, 2003.
25 Hancock, *John Gorton*, p. 2.
26 Ibid., pp. 1-2.
27 Ibid., p. 11
28 Ibid., p. 8.
29 Trengrove, *John Grey Gorton*, p. 26.
30 Don Whitington, *Twelfth Man?* Jacaranda. Brisbane, 1972, p, 122.
31 Hancock, *John Gorton*, p.7
32 Ibid., p. 19.
33 Gerard Henderson, "Sir John Grey Gorton," in Michelle Grattan, (ed), *Australian Prime Ministers*, New Holland, Sydney, 2000.
34 Trengrove, *John Grey Gorton,* p. 29.
35 Hancock, *John Gorton*, p. 20.
36 Trengrove, *John Grey Gorton,* p. 37.
37 Hancock, *John Gorton*, p. 22.
38 Ibid., p. 30.
39 Ibid., p. 32.
40 Alan Reid, *The Power Struggle*, Shakespeare Head, Sydney, 1969, p. 8.
41 Hancock, *John Gorton: He did it his* way, p. 37.
42 Reid, *The Gorton Experiment*, p. 9.
43 Garry McDonald as "Norman Gunston," cited in George Negus, *A Life: Sir John Gorton*, ABC TV, 1993.
44 Hancock, *John Gorton*, p. xiii.
45 Alan Elms, "Psychobiography and Case Study Methods," in R. W. Robins, R. C. Fraley and R. F. Krueger, (eds), *Handbook of Research Methods in Personality Psychology,* Guilford Press, Guilford Press, New York, 2007, pp. 97–113.

46 Harold Lasswell, *World Politics and Personal Insecurity*, McGraw-Hill, New York, 1935, pp. 154, 223.
47 Harold Laswell, *Power and Personality*, Norton, New York, 1948, pp. 33-39.
48 Ibid., p. 38.
49 James MacGregor Burns, *Leadership*, Harper and Row, New York, 1978, p. 61.
50 Nancy LaVerda, Andrea Vessey and William Waters, "Use of the Veterans History Project to Assess World War II Veterans' Perceptions of Military Experiences and Health," *Military Medicine*, Vol. 171, No. 11, 2006, pp. 1076-82.
51 Glen Elder, "War mobilization and the life course: A cohort of World War II veterans," *Sociological Forum*, Vol. 2, 1987, pp. 449–72.
52 Pim van Lommel, "Near-death experiences: the experience of the self as real and not as an illusion," *Annual New York Academy of Sciences*, Vol. 1234, 2011, pp. 1-10.
53 Gorton, cited in Hancock, *John Gorton: He did it his way*, p. 45.
54 Ibid., p. 49.
55 Geoffrey Browne, 'John Grey Gorton', *Biographical Dictionary of the Australian Senate*. https://biography.senate.gov.au/gorton-john-grey/
56 *Commonwealth Parliamentary Debates (CPD) Senate*, 1 March, 1950.
57 Paul Williams, "The Red Menace Fades," Unpublished Master of Arts thesis, Griffith University, Nathan, Brisbane, 1987.
58 *CPD Senate*, 7 June, 1950.
59 *CPD Senate*, 16 May, 1956.
60 *CPD Senate*, 19 June, 1956.
61 *CPD Senate*, 1 May, 1956.
62 *CPD Senate*, 7 June, 1956.
63 *CPD Senate*, 30 September, 1954.
64 *CPD Senate*, 29 October, 1952; 10 October, 1957.
65 Trengrove, *John Grey Gorton*, p. 118; Mungo MacCullum, *The Good, the Bad and the Unlikely: Australia's Prime Ministers*, Schwartz Publishing, Melbourne, 2014, p. 136.
66 Browne, "John Grey Gorton."
67 Hancock, *John Gorton*, p. 98. Trengrove, *John Grey Gorton*, p. 37.
68 Hancock, *John Gorton*, p. 100; Trengrove, *John Grey Gorton*, p. 37.
69 *CPD* Senate, 25 September 1963.
70 Hancock, *John Gorton*, p. 89. Trengrove, *John Grey Gorton*, p. 37.
71 Browne, "John Grey Gorton".
72 *CPD Senate*, 27 November 1959.

73 *CPD Senate*, 8 November 1962.
74 *CPD Senate*, 24 February 1959.
75 Athol Jones, *ABC of Politics*, 2nd ed., Cassell, Melbourne, 1973, p. 99.
76 John Howard, *The Menzies Era,* p. 313.
77 *CPD Senate*, 28 October 1966.
78 *CPD Senate*, 28 September 1967.
79 Hancock, *John Gorton*, p. 97. Trengrove, *John Grey Gorton,* p. 37.
80 Hancock, *John Gorton*, p. 122. Trengrove, *John Grey Gorton,* p. 37.
81 Personal communication with the author, 1998.
82 Hancock, *John Gorton*, p. 128. Trengrove, *John Grey Gorton,* p. 37.
83 *CPD Senate*, 25 October 1967.
84 Hancock, *John Gorton*, pp. 145-46. Trengrove, *John Grey Gorton,* p. 37.
85 MacCallum, "A Larrikin in the Lodge."
86 Hancock, *John Gorton*, p. 141. Trengrove, *John Grey Gorton,* p. 37.
87 Troy Bramston, "He raised a glass but not the bar," *The Australian*, 9 January 2018, p. 10.
88 Ibid., p. 425.
89 Abraham Maslow, "A Theory of Human Motivation," *Psychological Review*, Vol. 50, 1943, pp. 370-96.
90 Maslow, "A Theory of Human Motivation," pp. 370-96.
91 Graham Little, *Political Ensembles: A Psychological Approach to Politics and Leadership*, Oxford University Press, Melbourne, 1985, p. 9.
92 Ibid.
93 Ibid.
94 Ibid., p. 152.
95 Ibid., pp. 139-53.
96 Ibid., p. 136.
97 Max Walsh, *Poor Little Rich Country: The Path to the Eighties*, Penguin, Ringwood, p. 32.
98 *Financial Times*, 7 January 1969.
99 Personal communication with the author, 1998.
100 Peter Tiver, *The Liberal Party: Principles and Performance*, Jacaranda, Brisbane, 1978, pp. 238-39.
101 Trengrove, *John Grey Gorton*, Author's Note.
102 James Jupp, *Party Politics, 1966-81*, Allen and Unwin, Sydney, 1982, p. 54.
103 Ibid., p. 52.
104 Personal communication with the author, 1998.
105 Personal communication with the author, 1998.
106 *Commonwealth Parliamentary Debates (CPD) House of Representatives (HR)*, 19 September 1968.

107 *CPD HR*, 21 August, 26 August,1970.
108 Malcolm Abbott and Chris Doucouliagos, *The Changing Structure of Higher Education in Australia, 1949-2003*, School of Accounting, Economics and Finance Working Papers – Series 2003 SWP 2003/07 https://www.deakin.edu.au/__data/assets/pdf_file/0006/402594/swp2003_07.pdf
109 John Gorton, House of Representatives election campaign speech, 9 October, 1969, Museum of Australian Democracy, Canberra. https://electionspeeches.moadoph.gov.au/speeches/1969-john-gorton
110 John Gorton, Senate election campaign speech, 18 November 1970, *PM Transcripts*, Department of Prime Minister and Cabinet https://pmtranscripts.pmc.gov.au/release/transcript-2325
111 *CPD HR*, 21 August 1969.
112 *CPD HR*, 15 March 1971.
113 *CPD HR*, 21 August 1969.
114 Hancock, *John Gorton*, p. 185.
115 Hancock, *John Gorton*, p. 181.
116 Coral Dow and John Gardiner-Garden, *Overview of Indigenous Affairs: Part 1: 1901 to 1991 10 May 2011*, Parliament of Australia, Canberra. https://www.aph.gov.au/about_parliament/parliamentary_departments/parliamentary_library/pubs/bn/1011/indigenousaffairs1
117 Wallace Brown, *Ten Prime Ministers: Life Among the Politicians*, Longueville, Double Bay, 2002, p. 88.
118 National Archives of Australia (NAA), Cabinet Minute - Northern Territory - Land for "Gurindji" People. Series Q5872, Decision No. 203.
119 Matthew 5:48; Hancock, *John Gorton*, p. 106.
120 Hancock, *John Gorton*, p. 395. Trengrove, *John Grey Gorton*, p. 37.
121 NAA, Cabinet Minute – Commonwealth Grants Towards the Cost of State Assistance for Deserted Wives etc with Children, Series No. A5872, Decision No. 80.
122 *CPD Senate*, 7 November 1962.
123 *CPD HR*, 10 September 1969.
124 *CPD HR*, 5 March 1970.
125 *CPD HR*, 26 August 1969.
126 Keith Jackson, "Best of our new years: Gorton was packin' heat in Rabaul," *PNG Attitude*, 1 January, 2019.https://asopa.typepad.com/asopa_people/2019/01/best-of-our-new-years-gorton-was-packin-heat-in-rabaul.html
127 *CPD HR*, 18 October 1973.

128 NAA, Cabinet Minute - National Wage Case 1968, Series No. A5872, Decision No. 423.
129 Brian Carroll, *Australia's Prime Ministers: From Barton to Howard*, Rosenberg Publishing, Sydney, 2004, p. 216.
130 *CPD HR*, 25 February 1969.
131 Peter Golding, *Black Jack McEwen: Political Gladiator*, Melbourne University Press, Carlton, 1996, pp. 300-01.
132 *Morgan Gallup* Poll No. 200, 19 October 1968.
133 *Current Notes*, Vol. 40, No. 9, September 1969, p. 520.
134 *CPD HR*, 15 May, 1968.
135 *Morgan Gallup* Polls, No. 201, 21 December 1968, and No. 203, 18 April, 1969.
136 NAA, Legislation Committee – Cabinet Minute – Copyright Bill 1968, Series No. A5872, Decision No. 261/LEG.
137 Hancock, *John Gorton*, p. 257; see also NAA, Cabinet Minute - F111 Aircraft. Series No. A5872, Decision No. 124. Trengrove, *John Grey Gorton*, p. 37.
138 *CPD HR*, 10 September 1968.
139 Trengrove, *John Grey Gorton*, p. 13.
140 Tony Parkinson, "John Gorton: My Place in History," *Weekend Australian*, 'Review,' 1 February, 1994, p. 4.
141 Gorton, "Liberal Party: Attitudes and Policies," p. 322.
142 Personal communication with the author, 1998.
143 *CPD HR*, 15 May 1970.
144 Howard, *The Menzies Era*, p. 136.
145 *CPD HR*, 22 August 1968.
146 Hancock, *John Gorton*, p. 101.
147 Ibid., pp. 145-46
148 Personal communication with the author, 1998.
149 James L. Richardson, "Problems in Australian Foreign Policy," *Australian Journal of Politics and History*, Vol. 16, No. 1, 1970, p. 5.
150 *CPD HR*, 14 August 1969.
151 Personal communication with the author, 1998.
152 Edward S. K. Fung and Colin Mackerras, *From Fear to Friendship*, UQP, St. Lucia, 1986, p. 66; NAA Series No. A1838, 719/10/6 Part 7.
153 "Prime Minister Gorton of Australia visits Washington," *United States' Department of State Bulletin*, Vol. 60, 26 May 1969, p. 438.
154 Hancock, *John Gorton*, p. 151
155 Personal communication with the author, 1998.
156 Hubert Opperman, *Pedals, Politics, and People*, Haldane Publishing, Sydney, 1977, p. 496.

157 Peter Howson, *The Howson Diaries*, Viking Penguin, Ringwood, 1984, p. 435.
158 Paul Hasluck, *The Chance of Politics*, p. 174.
159 Reid, *The Gorton Experiment*, pp. 10; 31.
160 Personal communication with the author, 1998.
161 Reid, *The Gorton Experiment*, p. 14.
162 James Killen, *Killen: Inside Australian Politics*, Mandarin, Melbourne, 1989, p. 127.
163 Billy Snedden and Bernie Schedvin, *An Unlikely Liberal*, Macmillan, Melbourne, 1990, p. 83.
164 Colin Hughes, *Mr Prime Minister*, Oxford University Press, Melbourne, 1976, p. 186.
165 Gorton, cited in *The Bulletin*, 25 October 1969, p. 26.
166 Reid, *The Gorton Experiment*, pp. 56-57; 291.
167 *The Bulletin*, 26 October 1968, p. 17.
168 Neal Blewett and Dean Jaensch, *Playford to Dunstan: Politics of Transition*, Cheshire, Melbourne, 1971, p. 95.
169 *The Bulletin*, 18 October 1969, p. 28.
170 Snedden and Schedvin, *An Unlikely Liberal*, p. 87.
171 Clem Lloyd, *Parliament and the Press*, Melbourne University Press, Carlton, 1988, p. 245.
172 Hughes, *Mr Prime Minister*, p. 186.
173 Hancock, *John Gorton*, p. 207.
174 Rodney Tiffen, *News & Power*, Allen and Unwin, Sydney, 1989, p. 1.
175 Geoffrey Bolton, personal communication with the author, 1991.
176 Gorton, "The role of the PM," p. 454.
177 Personal communication with the author, 1998.
178 Patrick Weller, *Cabinet Government in Australia, 1901-2006*, UNSW Press, Sydney, p. 118.
179 See NAA *Cabinet Document Series* A5872.
180 The most commonly cited examples of Menzies 'deposed' rivals includes Richard (later Lord) Casey (on two occasions, 1940 and 1965), Percy Spender (1951), Eric Harrison (1956), Howard Beale (1958) and Garfield Barwick (1964). See Gerard Henderson, *Menzies' Child: The Liberal Party of Australia, 1944-1994*, Allen and Unwin, Sydney, 1994.
181 Personal communication with the author, 1998.
182 Weller, *Cabinet Government in Australia, 1901-2006*, p. 119.
183 Reid, *The Gorton* Experiment, pp. 79; 158-59.
184 Tiver, *The Liberal Party*, p. 238.
185 Personal communication with the author, 2001.
186 Patrick Weller, "Prime Ministers and Cabinet," in Patrick Weller,

(ed), *Menzies to Keating: The Development of the Australian Prime Ministership*, Melbourne University Press, Carlton, 1998, p. 7.
187   Museum of Australian Democracy, "John Gorton." https://primeministers.moadoph.gov.au/prime-ministers/john-gorton
188   Hancock, *John Gorton*, p. 170.
189   Clive Turnbull and Marjorie Tipping, *A Concise History of Australia*, Currey O'Neill, Melbourne, 1983, p. 190.
190   Bramston, "He raised a glass but not the bar."
191   Browne, "John Grey Gorton."
192   Personal communication with the author, 2000.
193   Hasluck, *The Chance of Politics*, pp. 174-75.
194   St John, *A Time to Speak*, p. 4.
195   Ibid., p. 151.
196   Graham Freudenberg, *A Certain Grandeur*, Penguin, Ringwood, 1987, p. 121.
197   Personal communication with the author, 2000.
198   Hancock, *John Gorton*, p. 170.
199   Mungo MacCullum, "A Larrkin in the Lodge," in Matthew Ricketson, (ed), *The Best Australian Profiles*, Black Inc, Melbourne, 2004, p. 364.
200   Damien Murphy, "Gentleman John fell on his sword," *Sydney Morning Herald*, 21 May 2002.
201   MacCullum, "A Larrkin in the Lodge," p. 369.
202   Ian Hancock, *Ainsley Gotto*, Connor Court, Redland Bay, 2020, pp. 10-11.
203   Ibid., pp. 173-74.
204   Hancock, *John Gorton*, p. 170.
205   Brian Carroll, *From Barton to Fraser*, Cassell, Sydney, 1979, p. 144.
206   Hancock, *John Gorton*, p. 215.
207   Ibid., p. 148.
208   Ibid., p. 248.
209   Ian McAllister, Malcolm Mackerras, Alvaro Ascui and Susan Moss, (eds), *Australian Political Facts*, Longman Cheshire, Melbourne, 1990, p. 98.
210   Hancock, *John Gorton*, pp. 322-24.
211   Howard, *The Menzies Era*, p. 557.
212   John Gorton, "I did it my way," *The Sunday Australian*, 8 August-12 September 1971.
213   Hancock, *John Gorton*, p. 365.
214   Ibid., p. 369.
215   Brett, *Australian Liberals and the Moral Middle Class*, pp. 158-59.
216   Browne, "John Grey Gorton."

217 Hancock, *John Gorton*, p. 388.
218 Ibid., p. 394.
219 Personal communication with the author, 1998.
220 Gough Whitlam, *The Whitlam Government, 1972-1975*, Penguin, Ringwood, 1985.

www.ingramcontent.com/pod-product-compliance
Lightning Source LLC
Chambersburg PA
CBHW070936160426
43193CB00011B/1698

NOAA's hams, shams, and scams

This book describes in depth the circumstances surrounding the loss of the nineteenth-century survey vessel *Robert J. Walker*, and some of the unscrupulous activities of the National Oceanic and Atmospheric Administration, which helped to identify a rusting carcass off the coast of Atlantic City, New Jersey as the remains of this sidewheel steamer, whose sinking precipitated the demise of twenty crew members.

Known to anglers and divers as the $25 Wreck and Mason's Paddle Wheeler, the rotting hull has been a popular fishing and diving site since as far back as the 1950's, perhaps earlier.

By their very nature, shipwreck stories have a dark side that involves death and destruction, heroism and cowardice, the luck of the draw, and the struggle for survival. The loss of the *Robert J. Walker* was no exception.

This volume relates in detail the contemporaneous happenstances that involved the construction, survey work, and loss of the *Robert J. Walker*, as well as current events, and the ominous future that the wreck and NOAA portend for American citizens in a climate in which individual freedom suffers from severe and sinister erosion.

Some of this saga is good, some of it is bad, and some is flagrantly ugly. The story is worth relating in depth so that people will understand the past, present, and ominous future of shipwreck discovery and exploration.

This book includes a dip into the seamy side of NOAA, which has been pulling the wool over America's eyes for decades. NOAA laid claim to the wreck in order to draw attention to itself. Worse than that, the obvious extortion was a foot in the door to laying specious claims not only to nearby shipwrecks, but eventually to every wreck off the American eastern seaboard.

NOAA's demand for territorial expansion is worse than the Fuhrer's. It has been going on surreptitiously against the will of the public. NOAA has been trying for years to take over all the submerged lands off the coasts of Massachusetts and North Carolina, with an eye to stitching them together off the intermediate States. Already a scheme is afoot to create a new National Marine Sanctuary in New Jersey waters: another nail in the coffin of liberty and the American way.

The *Robert J. Walker* was but a stepping stone toward NOAA's totalitarian rule: a wayward path of using and abusing those who died at sea as a means to achieve an autocratic end in which NOAA must reign supreme.

The good side of this story is the way in which recreational divers paved the way to the wreck's identification, and then were solely responsible for examining and mapping the site. These hard-working volunteers received no payment for their services. They did it for their love of exploring shipwrecks. Because of their dedication, the $25 Wreck alias Mason's Paddle Wheeler alias *Robert J. Walker* has risen from a lowly hulk at the bottom of the sea to a place of status in human consciousness.

Extra! Extra! Read all about it. From design to demise, from lost to found, from identification to detailed site descriptions, this book tells the story in its entirety . . .

. . . and then some.

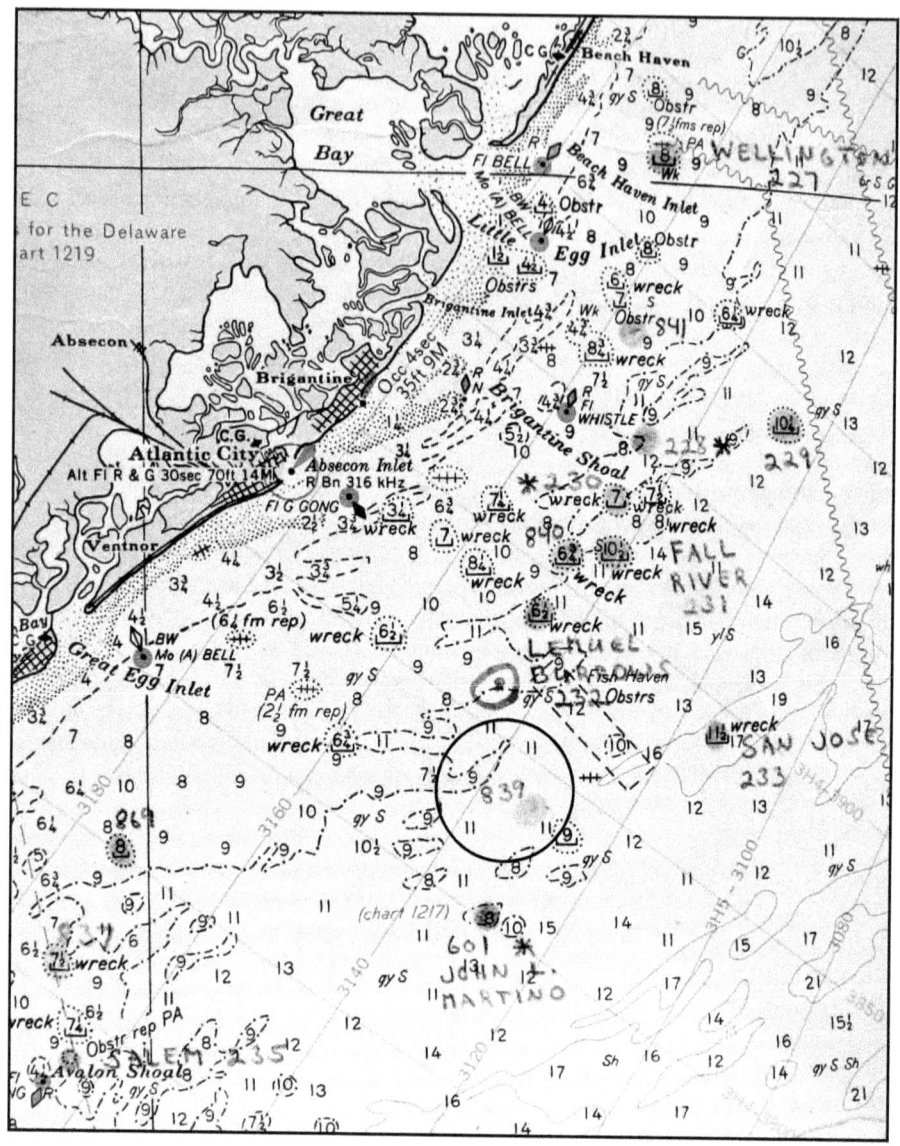

GPS numbers for the *Robert J. Walker* (alias $25 Wreck, alias Mason's Paddle Wheeler) Atlantic City, New Jersey:

39-13.230 / 74-17.269

Above is shown my offshore loran-A chart from the 1970's. Within the black circle I originally marked Wreck No. 839 from the 1944 *Gentian* Survey (the faint circular smudge below the "9"). *Gentian* surveyors used land ranges or sextant sightings to triangulate and calculate the position. Modern means of location place the wreck in the center of the "3" in "839," less than a quarter mile away.